God
to
Go

Delivering a Portable Celebration of Faith,
Inspiration, and Grace

James Stuart Bell and Tracy Macon Sumner

Adams Media
Avon, Massachusetts

Published by Adams Media, an F+W Publications Company
57 Littlefield Street
Avon, MA 02322
www.adamsmedia.com

ISBN 10: 1-59337-604-9
ISBN 13: 978-1-59337-604-8

Printed in Canada

J I H G F E D C B A

Library of Congress Cataloging-in-Publication Data
available from publisher

This publication is designed to provide accurate and authorita-
tive information with regard to the subject matter covered. It is
sold with the understanding that the publisher is not engaged in
rendering legal, accounting, or other professional advice. If legal
advice or other expert assistance is required, the services of a com-
petent professional person should be sought.
> —From a *Declaration of Principles* jointly adopted by
> a Committee of the American Bar Association and
> a Committee of Publishers and Associations

This book is available at quantity discounts
for bulk purchases.
For information, please call 1-800-872-5627.

Unless otherwise indicated, Scripture quotations are from
The Holy Bible, New International Version (NIV) © 1973, 1984
by International Bible Society, used by permission of Zondervan
Publishing House.

Interior image © JupiterImages

Contents

Preface

We live in a culture where there are great demands on our time. Between work, family, and other commitments, it can be difficult to find time to read your Bible and pray. Yet, we see in the Bible that God is to be our number-one priority when it comes to everything about our lives: our time, our affections, and even our money.

Andrew Murray (1828–1917), a Dutch Reformed minister who preached, taught, and wrote in South Africa, once wrote, "It is a glorious thing to get to know God in a new way in the inner chamber. It is something still greater and more glorious to know God as the all-sufficient One and to wait on His Spirit to open our hearts and minds wide to receive the great things, the new things which He really longs to bestow on those who wait for Him."

God truly does want to continually show us new things about Himself and to open us up to receive great things from Him. That is the nature of the generosity of our heavenly Father, and it's a promise found in His written Word, the Bible.

More than anything, God wants us to know Him—to know of His character and His attributes as they are repeatedly laid out for us in the Bible—and to know about the kinds of blessings He wants to pour out on us.

Our purpose in writing *God to Go* is to show you ways you can get to know God better so you can receive the blessings He has in store for you.

It is our hope that this book will help you in the study of the character of God by giving you bite-size snippets—readings that will take no more than ten minutes out of your day—of what God's Word has to say about His character and attributes.

The purpose of this book is not to take the place of regular personal Bible study and meditation. Instead, it is our hope that you will use this book during the course of your busy day to help you along in studying the Bible topically and, in the process, know God better. For example, if you read a section in this book on the grace of God, you can now go to your concordance and do a biblical study on the word *grace*. And if you read a section about His faithfulness, you can then go and do a study on the word *faithful*.

We serve a wonderful God who wants us to know Him more and more intimately and to become more and more like His Son, Jesus Christ. As you read this book, you'll see snapshots of the character of God, and you'll learn some of the things you can do to become the kind of believer He wants you to be.

Part 1

Grace

Open Yourself to Grace

"Our sense of the grace of God, of our neediness in the face of His omnipotent love, is a true barometer of genuine spirituality and biblical worship."

—Timothy George

One day, the evangelist Billy Graham was driving when a police officer stopped him and informed him he had been speeding. Graham immediately admitted his guilt, but the officer gave him a ticket.

When Graham appeared in traffic court, the judge asked, "Guilty, or not guilty?" Graham pleaded guilty, and the judge replied, "That'll be ten dollars— a dollar for every mile you went over the limit."

When the judge recognized that it was Billy Graham standing before him, he said, "You have violated the law. The fine must be paid, but I am going to pay it for you." Then he took Graham out and bought him a steak dinner.

"That," Graham later said, "is how God treats repentant sinners!"[1]

The way God treats repentant sinners can be summed up in one word: grace.

Grace has been defined as God doing for us what we don't deserve and can't do for ourselves. Salvation and forgiveness of our sin certainly fits in that category.

On our own, there is nothing we can do to make ourselves acceptable to a righteous God. Each of us, no matter how hard we try to live a good life, is a sinner in need of a way to God. But He provided that way, sending His Son Jesus Christ as a once-and-for-all sacrifice for our sin. Much like the judge who paid Billy Graham's traffic ticket, God Himself has paid the price for our sin, making it possible for us to have fellowship with Him. The apostle Paul summed up the relationship between God's grace and our salvation like this: "For it is by grace you have been saved, through faith—and this not from yourselves, it is the gift of God—not by works, so that no one can boast." (Ephesians 2:8–9)

✝ Faith in Action

God's grace is the source and assurance of everything we have in Him. It's the picture of a God who does everything for us, infinitely beyond what we could ever deserve or earn.

Enjoy Your Access to God

*"God does not stand afar off as I struggle to speak.
He cares enough to listen with more than casual
attention. He translates my scrubby words and hears
what is truly inside. He hears my sighs and uncertain
gropings as fine prose."*

—Timothy Jones

Our lives today are filled with access codes—codes for our computers, bank accounts, and telephones. Having the right access codes can make life a lot easier, and if we don't have the right codes, our lives can become quite complicated.

Many people go through times of frustration because they feel that they somehow don't have the right "access code" when it comes to approaching God.

In his book *The Supremacy of Jesus*, author Stephen Neill points out that the word *access* appears in only three New Testament passages—(Romans 5:1–2, Ephesians 2:18, and Ephesians 3:12) and that these passages teach us four things about our faith:

1. We have access into grace. (Romans 5:2) God's throne is the throne of grace. (Hebrews 4:16)

2. We have access unto the Father. (Ephesians 2:18) Though He is sovereign, we can still approach Him as a child does a father. (Luke 11:11–13; Romans 8:15)

3. We have access through Jesus Christ. (1 Timothy 2:5) The blood gives us boldness. (Hebrews 10:19)

4. We have access by our faith. (Romans 5:2; Ephesians 3:12) The essential ingredient is prayer. (Hebrews 10:22)[2]

The writer of Hebrews said this of our access to God: " . . . let us draw near to God with a sincere heart in full assurance of faith, having our hearts sprinkled to cleanse us from a guilty conscience and having our bodies washed with pure water." (Hebrews 10:22)

In other words, because we have been purified through Jesus Christ on the cross, we can know that when we make an active decision to draw near to God, He will draw near to us.

✝ Faith in Action

God is not some distant, disinterested Creator but a loving heavenly Father who wants to draw us into the life He offers by allowing us full access to Himself.

Abide in God

*"The times we find ourselves having to wait on others
may be the perfect opportunities to train ourselves to
wait on the Lord."*

—Joni Eareckson Tada

The life of Saint Patrick, the fifth-century missionary to Ireland who became known as the Apostle
to the Irish, left behind a beautiful prayer of devotion
to God titled "The Lorica of St. Patrick." Here is an
excerpt from that prayer:

> *I bind to myself today*
> *God's Power to guide me,*
> *God's Might to uphold me,*
> *God's Wisdom to teach me,*
> *God's Eye to watch over me,*
> *God's Ear to hear me. . .*

This prayer reflects St. Patrick's obedience to the
command of Jesus Christ: that His disciples, "Abide
in Me, and I in you. As the branch cannot bear fruit
of itself, unless it abides in the vine, neither can you,

unless you abide in Me." (John 15:4 NEW KING JAMES VERSION)

The Bible tells us that we are to find rest in God and that we are to wait for Him, but that doesn't mean resting idly. Jesus' words in John 15:4 are translated in a different version of the Bible as, "Remain in me, and I will remain in you."

The Bible tells us repeatedly that we are to abide in God and in His Word. And how do we do that? The apostle John wrote, "Now he who keeps His commandments abides in Him, and He in him. And by this we know that He abides in us, by the Spirit whom He has given us." (1 John 3:24 NKJV)

There is no simple ten-step key to abiding in God; it's as simple as living a life where we continually listen to Him, speak to Him, and obey Him—three things that are intertwined to the point where we can't do one without doing the other two.

✝ Faith in Action

God desires to bless each and every one of us first with His presence and then with the things we need to live lives pleasing to Him. In order to receive those blessings, we need to do one thing: Abide in Him!

Honor the Perfection of Christ

"The essence of temptation is the invitation to live independently of God."

—Neil Anderson

As the Union Pacific Railroad was being constructed, workers built a bridge across a canyon. The builder loaded a train with enough equipment to double its normal payload and then drove the train to the middle of the bridge, where it stayed an entire day. One worker asked, "Are you trying to break this bridge?" "No," the builder replied, "I'm trying to prove that the bridge won't break."[3]

Jesus had to show Himself worthy to bear the sins of the world by proving that He could withstand the devil's temptations.

The Bible tells us that no sooner had Jesus been baptized and had the voice of His Father affirm His identity for all to hear than the Spirit of God Himself led the Son into the wilderness. There He would spend forty days and nights fasting and praying—and being tempted.

The devil knew that if He could entice Jesus into just one sin, he could derail the plan of salvation. Three times the devil came at Jesus with temptations that are common to all of us, and three times Jesus resisted the temptation and repelled the devil by telling him, "It is written. . . . "

Jesus was probably at His most vulnerable that day. He had gone without food for almost six weeks, and His body was aching for nourishment. But Jesus had immersed Himself in the written Word of God and had also spent time in One-on-One communion with the Father.

Now, after spending forty days of prayer and fasting, Jesus was ready. Satan pulled out all the stops in trying to coax Jesus into sin, even promising Him all the kingdoms of the world if He would just bow down to the devil.

But Jesus knew these things were not part of God's program for His life. He knew that the Father wanted Him to be the Lamb without blemish (1 Peter 1:19) who while He was tempted in every way we are, never gave in to sin.

† Faith in Action

Jesus was the one man of whom we can rightly say, "in him is no sin." (1 John 3:5)

The High Cost of God's Free Gift

"It is true, Christian, the debt you owe to God must be paid in good and lawful money, but, take comfort. Here Christ is the paymaster."
—William Gurnall

Rodney "Gypsy" Smith (1860–1947) was a powerful preacher who influenced the lives of millions of people. After his conversion in 1876, he joined the Salvation Army and served as an officer in that organization until 1882. After that, he began working as a traveling evangelist with organizations all over the world.

A few days after Smith became a Christian, an old man asked Smith if he had trusted Jesus and nothing else for his salvation. "I cannot trust myself," Smith replied, "for I am nothing. I cannot trust what I have, for I have nothing. I cannot trust what I know, for I know nothing."

Smith stands as an example of someone who understood that his salvation was based on the goodness and graciousness of God.

Sadly, many people—including many, many professing Christians—have a mixed-up idea of what it takes to be saved. They believe that they earn their salvation by being a good person or through doing good deeds.

While those things are outward evidence of a person's salvation, they are not what saves us. The Bible tells us that salvation is a free gift of God to people who don't deserve it. While God's offer of salvation is free, the salvation itself was anything but. It cost Him *everything*. It cost the Father the sacrifice of His only Son and cost the Son the humiliation of dying an awful death on a cross of wood. And He did those things not because we are good or worthy but because we owed Him a debt for our sins we could never pay.

Jesus said, "God so loved the world that he gave his one and only Son, that whoever believes in him shall not perish but have eternal life." (John 3:16) His mission on earth was to provide a way to salvation and fellowship with God.

✝ Faith in Action
Salvation came at a price God was willing to pay on behalf of everyone who would put their faith in Him.

Visualize Our God of All Eternity

"Nothing can separate you from God's love, absolutely nothing. God is enough for time, God is enough for eternity. God is enough!"

—Hannah Whitall Smith

Skeptics through the ages have posed the question (or variations of it), "If God created the universe and the world we live in, then who created God?"

The problem with this question, no matter how honestly it is asked, is that it presupposes that God is like us in that He has a beginning and that there was a time when there not only wasn't a cosmos and the earth we live on but that there wasn't a God to create those things.

The Bible speaks very clearly of God's eternal nature. The psalmist wrote of a God who is "from everlasting to everlasting," (Psalm 57:15) and the prophet Isaiah wrote of the one true God who "inhabits eternity." (Isaiah 57:15) We also read of God being called *El Olam*, which when translated from Hebrew to English literally means "The Everlasting God." (See Genesis 21:33.)

Why is it so hard for the human mind to grasp the idea of a God who lives in eternity past and will live on for eternity future? Because God has limited our knowledge by creating us to live within the bounds of time. For that reason, it is no more possible for us to fully grasp the idea of an eternal God than it is for us to fully know what it would be like to live our lives as a planet. We may have a small inkling, but we'll never understand what it is like to live outside the bounds of time.

Time exists only within the created universe and since God is not a "created" being, He has no past or future but only an eternal present.

✝ Faith in Action

God is the one and only eternal being; He has no beginning and no end. And while we humans are not eternal beings in that we've always been, when we put our faith in Jesus Christ, we are promised an eternity in the presence of an almighty God who will never stop pouring out His love on us.

Part 2

Courage

Courage from Above

> "Hope has two beautiful daughters. Their names are
> anger and courage: anger at the way things are and
> courage to see that they do not remain the way they are."
> —Augustine of Hippo

Dietrich Bonhoeffer was a World War II–era pastor and theologian in Germany who was arrested and imprisoned for assisting some Jews in their bid to escape Nazi Germany. Later, he was implicated in a plot to assassinate Hitler. On April 8, 1945, about two years after he was first imprisoned and just three days before Allied forces arrived, Hitler ordered Bonhoeffer hanged.

The Bible, in both the Old Testament and the New Testament, contains many stories of this kind of courage, including one in the fourth chapter of Acts. In this passage, the apostles Peter and John continued to preach the message of Jesus Christ despite the opposition of the religious leaders in Jerusalem.

Peter and John were arrested for their preaching, and the next day they were brought before the authorities to explain themselves and their actions.

But rather than keep quiet, Peter, filled with the Holy Spirit, told them very plainly that they had done their preaching and miracles through the power and authority of Jesus Christ.

Even though the religious authorities in Jerusalem opposed what Peter and John were doing, they were amazed at their courage: "When they saw the courage of Peter and John and realized that they were unschooled, ordinary men, they were astonished and they took note that these men had been with Jesus." (Acts 4:13)

When we walk with Jesus, He gives us courage—courage to speak the truth and to do what is right, even when it costs us personally.

Faith in Action

God wants us to understand that when He is with us, we have no reason to give in to fear. As He told His servant Joshua, He tells us, "Have I not commanded you? Be strong and courageous. Do not be terrified; do not be discouraged, for the Lord your God will be with you wherever you go." (Joshua 1:9)

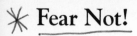

✳ Fear Not!

"Beloved, I say, let your fears go, lest they make you fainthearted. Stop inspiring fear in those around you and now take your stand in faith. God has been good and He will continue to manifest His goodness."
—Francis Frangipane

You probably don't have to think very long or hard to figure out what in this life really scares you. There are healthy kinds of fear. For example, most people react with fear at the thought of stepping out in the middle of a busy street. That kind of fear is healthy because it keeps us safe. Then there is the healthiest fear of all, the fear of God, which isn't fear in the dread or fright sense of the word but more of a healthy awe and reverence for our Creator.

Then there are also unhealthy fears—fear of criticism, opposition, failure, and the future, to name a few. These fears are unhealthy and hurtful because they keep us from being everything that God wants us to be and doing everything He wants us to do for Him.

In an October 4, 1857, sermon titled "Fear Not," famed British preacher Charles Haddon Spurgeon said this of these kinds of fear:

> Get rid of fear, because fear is painful. How it torments the spirit! When the Christian trusts, he is happy; when he doubts, he is miserable. When the believer looks to his Master and relies upon him, he can sing; when he doubts his Master, he can only groan.

God never intended for any of us to live a life of fear. Rather, He wants us to go boldly and confidently into the world around us, knowing that He is with us. As the psalmist King David wrote, "God is our refuge and strength, an ever-present help in trouble. Therefore we will not fear, though the earth give way and the mountains fall into the heart of the sea, though its waters roar and foam and the mountains quake with their surging." (Psalm 46:1–3)

✝ Faith in Action

Are you fearful of anything today? Then take a moment and think about how big and powerful the God you serve really is.

Sacrifice Yourself

> *"Self-preservation is the first law of nature,*
> *but self-sacrifice is the highest rule of grace."*
>
> —Anonymous

Angus McGillivray was a Scottish soldier in a World War II Japanese prison camp—notorious for its poor treatment of POWs—and an incredible example of self-sacrifice and how it can transform the world around us.

The prison camp where McGillivray was lodged was filled with Americans, Australians, and Brits who had helped build the bridge over the River Kwai. While these men had all been allies in the war with Japan, the conditions at the prison camp had helped create a situation where they would do anything—including stealing and cheating one another—in order to survive.

The Scottish soldiers were known for watching out for one another. In the prison camps, they would pair off as buddies, and each of these men made it their personal mission to make sure their buddies survived.

Angus's buddy was in trouble, so close to death that everyone but Angus had given up on him. Angus gave everything he had—his own blanket, his own food—to make sure his buddy recovered. Eventually, Angus's buddy recovered, but Angus himself paid the ultimate price. After Angus's death, doctors found out that the cause was starvation and exhaustion.

As the cause of Angus's death made its way around the camp, there was a remarkable change in attitude and action among the men. Where before it had been survival of the fittest, now men began focusing on the well-being of their comrades. They even began pooling their talents, and before long they had started an orchestra in which they played homemade instruments and a church called "Church Without Walls," which even some of the Japanese guards attended.[4]

Before He began His final journey to the Cross, Jesus told His disciples, "Greater love has no one than this; that one lay down his life for his friends." (John 15:13) Then that's exactly what He did so that they—as well as you—could live forever in God's presence.

✝ Faith in Action

God's love is a self-sacrificing kind of love, and it's the kind of love He calls us to demonstrate to others.

Suffer with Christ

"We all know people who have been made much meaner and more irritable and more intolerable to live with by suffering: it is not right to say that all suffering perfects. It only perfects one type of person . . . the one who accepts the call of God in Christ Jesus."
—Oswald Chambers

Polycarp (70–155) was the Christian bishop of Smyrna (modern-day Izmir, Turkey) in a time when being an outspoken Christian often meant death. The Roman emperors of that time had unleashed violent attacks against Christianity, which they saw as a dangerous cult that needed to be stopped.

Polycarp, who had been a disciple of the apostle John, was seized by Roman soldiers and ordered to deny Christ and swear an oath to Caesar. But he refused, instead declaring, "Eighty-six years I have served Christ, and He never did me any wrong. How can I blaspheme my King who saved me?" Because Polycarp refused to renounce his faith, he was burned at the stake.

It's hard to imagine a time and place where people were tortured or killed just because they were Christians. But the Bible makes it very clear that some who follow Jesus will suffer, but it's actually an honor to do so:

- "Now if we are children, then we are heirs—heirs of God and coheirs with Christ, if indeed we share in his sufferings in order that we may also share in his glory." (Romans 8:17)
- "For it has been granted to you on behalf of Christ not only to believe in him, but also to suffer for him." (Philippians 1:29)
- "Therefore I endure everything for the sake of the elect, that they too may obtain the salvation that is in Christ Jesus, with eternal glory. The path to glory is always through suffering." (2 Timothy 2:10)

✝ Faith in Action

Whatever we have to endure because of our faith in Jesus Christ—be it ridicule from coworkers, rejection by friends and family, or whatever this fallen world throws at us—we should, as the apostle Peter wrote, " . . . rejoice that you participate in the sufferings of Christ, so that you may be overjoyed when his glory is revealed." (1 Peter 4:13)

Seek the High Ground

"Wisdom is, and starts with, the humility to accept the fact that you don't have all the right answers, and the courage to learn to ask the right questions."

—Anonymous

In the movie *Bruce Almighty*, a reporter named Bruce Nolan complains to and about God because his life isn't going the way he thinks it should. Finally, God has heard enough of the complaining and gives Bruce the opportunity to be God for a time.

At first, Bruce demonstrates his power fairly harmlessly—starting his car with the word "Start!" (even though it has a dead battery), and potty training his previously unhousebroken dog. But soon, Bruce begins using his power selfishly by taking revenge on a rival and by manipulating news events so that he can get the scoop on other reporters.

In the end, Bruce realizes that he can't handle the job of being "God," even over the little things in his life, let alone over world events.

In truth, no one can handle the job of being God better than God Himself. He's the one who knows all, sees all, is all-powerful, and, most important, is all-loving. Even on our very best days, none of us is any of those things.

Speaking through the prophet Isaiah, God tells us, "' . . . my thoughts are not your thoughts, neither are your ways my ways,' declares the Lord. 'As the heavens are higher than the earth, so are my ways higher than your ways and my thoughts than your thoughts.'" (Isaiah 55:8–9)

When we feel the need or desire to question God or to doubt His wisdom in dealing with all our life situations—and those of others—we need to remember that our God sees things from an eternal and infinite perspective.

✠ Faith in Action

Because everything God does is motivated by His love for us and by His desire to see His own name glorified, we can rest in the fact that everything He allows or causes to happen will be, in the end, for our very best—and for the very best for a world He sent His Son to save.

Part 3

Joy

✳ True Contentment

"God cannot give us a happiness and peace apart from Himself, because it is not there. There is no such thing."
—C. S. Lewis

When we think of the word *contentment*, we tend to think of achieving and acquiring the things in life that will make us feel more fulfilled, comfortable, and successful. Many of us who feel discontentment believe with all our hearts that "if only" we could just achieve more, get more, and enjoy more, we would finally feel content and satisfaction. The biggest problem with "if only" thinking is that even when we receive or achieve what we thought would make us content, we want more.

Consider these words of the apostle Paul: "I have learned to be content whatever the circumstances. I know what it is to be in need, and I know what it is to have plenty." (Philippians 4:11–12)

Paul wrote his letter to the Philippian church, which he founded on one of his missionary journeys, while he was sitting in a Roman prison facing the distinct possibility that he was going to be executed simply because he was preaching the Gospel. But despite his own circumstances, he writes words of love, encouragement, optimism, comfort, and warmth to people who had things a lot better than he did.

It's difficult for most of us to figure out how someone living in such conditions could write such things. But in the second half of Philippians 4:12, Paul wrote how he did it: "I have learned the secret of being content in any and every situation."

The secret Paul learned was one we all need to discover for ourselves: Whether we have a little or a lot, whether we are living in comfort or in poverty, whether we are healthy or ill, we can be content because we have the privilege of knowing and serving a God who has promised to meet our every need, be it spiritual, emotional, or physical.

✝ Faith in Action

You should learn, as the apostle Paul did, that true contentment comes from a life devoted to loving and serving God and others.

Celebrate the Wonder
of the Trinity

*"Tell me how it is that in this room there are three
candles and but one light, and I will explain to you the
mode of the divine existence."*

—John Wesley

One of the most mysterious—and most wonderful—truths about our God is that He has
revealed Himself in the form of three distinct personalities: the Father, the Son, and the Holy Spirit. This
truth is what is called doctrine of the Trinity.

For centuries, Christians have wrestled with
coming up with an adequate illustration of the Trinity. Tertullian (160–220), a North African theologian
and defender of the Christian faith, likened the Trinity to a plant that yields beautiful flowers when he
wrote, "God the Father is a deep root, the Son is the
shoot that breaks forth into the world, and the Spirit
is that which spreads beauty and fragrance." In truth,
no analogy illustrates the Trinity perfectly.

Don't waste your time looking for the word Trinity in the Bible. But while the word doesn't appear,

the idea certainly does. The Bible teaches that there is one God who is represented by three distinct persons. (For example, Deuteronomy 6:4 says, "Hear, O Israel: The Lord our God, the Lord is one.")

One of the many Scripture passages that point to a triune is found in the Gospel of Matthew, which says, "As soon as Jesus was baptized, he went up out of the water. At that moment heaven was opened, and he saw the Spirit of God descending like a dove and lighting on him. And a voice from heaven said, 'This is my Son, whom I love; with him I am well pleased.'" Later, Jesus Himself commanded His disciples, "Therefore go and make disciples of all nations, baptizing them in the name of the Father and of the Son and of the Holy Spirit." (Matthew 28:19)

✝ Faith in Action

It is important for us to understand the truth of the Trinity because we need to have all of God, and in order to do that, we need to know the roles of each of these personalities in our own lives.

Be Joyful!

> *"The most valuable thing the Psalms
> do for me is to express the same delight in God
> which made David dance."*
> —C. S. Lewis

There are many definitions for the word *joy*. If you were to get out your thesaurus and look at synonyms for the word, you would find happiness, elation, pleasure, and delight. However, those words don't quite capture the true meaning of the joy of the Lord. That joy isn't based on our present circumstances or emotional states. The joy of the Lord is to be a constant in our lives, even when we face circumstances that might, if only temporarily, rob us of our happiness or pleasure.

The word *joy* (or variations of it) is found literally hundreds of times in the Bible—at least fifty-seven times in the New Testament alone. This tells us that we as believers are to live lives of joy. And we aren't to have inner joy just when it seems that our lives are blessed, or just when we aren't going through difficult times. The Bible tells us that we are to have the joy of the Lord within during the good times and during the difficult times alike.

We are to be joyful . . .

- . . . abundantly. (2 Corinthians 8:2)
- . . . constantly. (Philippians 4:4)
- . . . during times of sorrow. (2 Corinthians 6:10)
- . . . during times of trials. (James 1:2, 1 Peter 1:6)
- . . . in the midst of persecution. (Matthew 5:11–12, Luke 6:22–23, Hebrews 10:34)
- . . . when we are enduring calamities. (Habakkuk 3:17–18)

There are many reasons why God wants us to live lives filled with His joy. God wants us to be joyful because it glorifies Him and focuses people's attention to Him. And He wants us to be joyful because it benefits us.

✝ Faith in Action

The apostle Paul wrote that we are to always have inner joy, even during difficult times: " . . . we also rejoice in God through our Lord Jesus Christ, through whom we have now received reconciliation." (Romans 5:11)

Enjoy True Spiritual Riches

"Satan promises the best, but pays with the worst . . .
But God pays as he promises;
all his payments are made in pure gold."
—Thomas Brooks

The story goes that about two hundred years ago, workers opened the tomb of the great conqueror Charlemagne and saw a startling sight. There was Charlemagne's body in a sitting position, clothed in the finest kingly garments, with a scepter in his bony hand. On his knee lay a copy of the Bible, with his lifeless finger pointing to this verse: "For what shall it profit a man, if he shall gain the whole world, and lose his own soul?" (Mark 8:36)

This story demonstrates something all believers need to understand: that we are to put the pursuit of earthly riches and power far behind our pursuit of spiritual riches and the pursuit of God's kingdom.

The apostle Paul wrote to a young pastor named Timothy, "But godliness with contentment is great gain. For we brought nothing into the world, and we can take nothing out of it. But if we have food and clothing, we will be content with that." (1 Timothy 6:6–8) Paul went on to tell Timothy, "But you, man of God, flee from all this [materialism], and pursue righteousness, godliness, faith, love, endurance and gentleness."

Paul's message to Timothy is still fresh and relevant to believers today. Paul wanted Timothy to remember that he was to put the pursuit of earthly riches well behind his pursuit of spiritual riches, the kind of riches Jesus had come to bring. In doing that, he would find true contentment.

When we pursue earthly riches, we may find happiness, but it will be a temporary happiness, one with no eternal significance. But when we pursue Jesus Christ, we receive many benefits of spiritual riches, including . . .

- . . . absolution from all charges. (Acts 13:39)
- . . . a position. (Ephesians 2:6)
- . . . redemption. (Romans 3:25)
- . . . salvation. (Romans 5:10)[5]

✠ Faith in Action

Earthly riches will all pass away, but the riches we lay up for ourselves with God will last for eternity.

God: Our Reason for Optimism

> *"I belong to the 'Great-God Party,' and will have*
> *nothing to do with the 'Little-God Party.'*
> *Christ does not want nibblers of the possible,*
> *but grabbers of the impossible."*
>
> —C. T. Studd

There's an anonymously written and fairly well-known poem that demonstrates the value of having an attitude of optimism, even in the face of what looks like overwhelming—if not hopeless—odds:

> *I passed a sand lot yesterday,*
> *Some kids were playing ball.*
> *I strolled along the third base line*
> *Within the fielder's call.*
>
> *"Say, what's the score?" I asked.*
> *He yelled to beat the stuffing,*
> *"There's no one out, the bases full,*
> *They're winning forty-two to nothing!"*

"You're getting beat, aren't you my friend?"
And then in no time flat
He answered, "No, sir, not as yet!
Our side hasn't been up to bat!"

There's something wonderful about the simple faith of a child when it comes to doing the impossible. This is optimism in its purest—and most powerful—form. It illustrates and sometimes embodies childlike faith, the kind of faith that God best responds to.

The prophet Jeremiah, who lived in a very dark time, recorded this promise from God: "'For I know the plans that I have for you,' declares the Lord, 'plans for welfare and not for calamity to give you a future and a hope.'" (Jeremiah 29:11)

Optimism and faith are not the same things—not even close. Optimism is based in the hope that something good will come out of even the stickiest life situations, while faith is based in the absolute assurance that God is working to accomplish what is not humanly possible.

✝ Faith in Action

When we place our faith in the God who loves us and is concerned with every aspect of our lives, we have an attitude of optimism so strong that we know He'll come through for us, even in the face of what appears impossible.

Rejoice in the Resurrection

"Christ is risen! There is life, therefore, after death!
His resurrection is the symbol and pledge of
universal resurrection!"
—Henry Ward Beecher

If there is anything as important in the story of Jesus as the Cross, it's His resurrection. First Corinthians 15:14–15 tells us that Christ's resurrection is at the very heart of the Christian faith, that if He wasn't raised from the dead then our faith is worthless. Had Jesus remained in the grave, He would have left promises unfulfilled, meaning that He wasn't really the Messiah at all.

As Jesus warned the disciples, He was arrested in Jerusalem, then tried by religious *and* secular authorities and cruelly executed on a cross. After His burial, the disciples still hadn't grasped His promise that He would rise from the dead. To them, this movement they had joined was finished because their Master was now dead.

But on the third day after Jesus' death, several of His followers were eyewitnesses to something that proved beyond all doubt that He was everything He had claimed to be, and that was the empty grave. Later, Jesus removed all doubt about what had happened to Him when He appeared personally to all of them.

Jesus demonstrated His uniqueness when He rose from the dead. In a time when literally dozens of men had come on the scene proclaiming themselves the long-awaited Messiah, He set Himself apart. But while the others died and were never heard from again, Jesus lived.

And the world would never be the same again.

John of Damascus (675–749), an eighth-century theologian/writer/poet, wrote "The Day of Resurrection," a beautiful poem about the resurrection of Jesus Christ and what it means to those who believe in Him. The last stanza reads:

> *Let all things seen and unseen*
> *Their notes in gladness blend,*
> *For Christ the Lord hath risen,*
> *Our Joy that hath no end.*

✝ Faith in Action

Had Jesus not been raised from the dead, He would have been nothing more than a footnote in Jewish history. But because He lives, we can have forgiveness, eternal life, and God Himself.

Part 4

Forgiveness

Forgive, Sooner Rather than Later

"But forgiveness is not an emotion. . . . Forgiveness is an act of will, and the will can function regardless of the temperature of the heart."

—Corrie ten Boom

James Edward Oglethorpe, a general and philanthropist, became acquainted with John Wesley, the now-famous eighteenth-century missionary to Georgia. During one conversation with Wesley, Oglethorpe stated, "I never forgive, and I never forget." To that, Wesley replied, "Then, Sir, I hope you never sin."

John Wesley's point was simple: *Only those of us who are without sin have the privilege of continuing to hold the sins of others against them.* There was only one man who ever lived a sinless life, and His mission on earth was to bring forgiveness.

Jesus spoke many times about the importance of forgiving those whose words or actions cause us pain. He instructed His followers to, "Love your enemies and pray for those who persecute you" (Matthew 5:44) and warned them, " . . . if you forgive men when they sin against you, your heavenly Father will also forgive you. But if you do not forgive men their sins, your Father will not forgive your sins." (Matthew 6:14–15)

Jesus even went so far as to say that our forgiveness is to be unlimited. Peter, one of Jesus' closest disciples, asked Jesus how many times he should forgive someone who sins against him—should he put the limit at seven times? But Jesus answered, "I tell you, not seven times, but seventy-seven times." (See Matthew 18:21–22.)

The most wonderful example of forgiveness in the Bible was Jesus, who as He hung dying on a cross, a punishment He received though He was innocent of any crime, extended forgiveness to His executioners: "Father, forgive them, for they do not know what they are doing." (Luke 23:34)

✝ Faith in Action

Paul wrote of our primary motivation for forgiving others: "Be kind and compassionate to one another, forgiving each other, just as in Christ God forgave you." (Ephesians 4:32) In other words, we can't afford to hold back from others the same kind of forgiveness that God has so freely given us.

Bask in God's Unlimited Forgiveness

> *"Our wickedness shall not overpower the unspeakable goodness and mercy of God; our dullness shall not overpower God's wisdom, nor our infirmity God's omnipotence."*
>
> —John of Kronstadt

When an elderly gentlemen heard from his grandson that Jesus loved him and was willing to forgive even the worst of his sins, he had his doubts.

The man had done it all: As a youth, he lived a life of drinking and carousing. As a soldier in World War II, he did things he couldn't even talk about. As a middle-aged man, he cheated on his wife and in his business.

Now, as his teenaged grandson talked to him about the forgiveness of Jesus Christ, he couldn't believe it. It wasn't that he didn't want forgiveness and eternal life, and it wasn't that he didn't believe God had sent Jesus to be our Savior. The problem was that he couldn't believe that God wanted anything to do with someone like him. What he couldn't accept was that God's love and forgiveness know no bounds.

Even many believers have a difficult time believing that God has forgiven every sin they have ever committed. In the backs of their minds, there just has to be that one "biggie" that God is just waiting to drop the gavel over.

However, no sin is so grievous that it is beyond His ability to forgive. King David, himself a beneficiary of God's willingness to forgive even the worst offenses, wrote, " . . . he does not treat us as our sins deserve or repay us according to our iniquities. For as high as the heavens are above the earth, so great is his love for those who fear him; as far as the east is from the west, so far has he removed our transgressions from us." (Psalm 103:10–12)

✝ Faith in Action

We often hold on to offenses from the past, only to bring them up later when it's to our advantage. Not so with God. When we bring our sins to Him, He forgives us, cleanses us, and casts every wrong act we have committed or wrong thought we've had in our heads into a sea of forgetfulness.

Confess Now

"It is impossible for a man to be freed from the habit of sin before he hates it, just as it is impossible to receive forgiveness before confessing his trespasses."

—Ignatius of Loyola

One morning four preachers met to confess their sins to each other.

Three of the preachers confessed their sins and waited for the fourth preacher to 'fess up. He was quiet, so one of his friends said, "Come on, now! The rest of us have all confessed, and it's your turn now." Preacher number four replied, "Well, my sin is gossip. In fact, I can't wait to get out of here!"

Unfortunately, the fourth preacher lacked what the Bible calls repentance, meaning turning away from his sin of gossip. King Solomon addressed this when he wrote, "He who conceals his sins does not prosper, but whoever confesses and renounces them finds mercy." (Proverbs 28:13)

Jesus illustrated God's unfailing willingness to forgive a repentant sinner when He told the parable of the prodigal son, a story of a young man who left the security of his father's estate and blew his inheritance on fast living. When the money ran out, he was so destitute that he had to take a job feeding a farmer's pigs.

Finally, the young man had enough. He swallowed his pride, went back to his father, and told him, "Father, I have sinned against heaven and against you. I am no longer worthy to be called your son," (Luke 15:21) then asked if he could stay in his father's home . . . as a hired hand.

The father wouldn't hear of it. He ordered the servants to set up a party for his son, because " . . . this son of mine was dead and is alive again; he was lost and is found." (Luke 15:24)

Jesus pointed out to His disciples that our Father in heaven is just like the father in the parable. When we come to Him and confess our sins, He is, as the apostle John wrote, "faithful and just and will forgive us our sins and purify us from all unrighteousness." (1 John 1:9)

✝ Faith in Action

Confession is the one and only way to find forgiveness and cleansing from our sin.

Part 5

Patience

Accept It When God Says No

> "We forget that God sometimes has to say No.
> We pray to Him as our heavenly Father, and like wise
> human fathers, He often says, No, not from whim or
> caprice, but from wisdom and from love, and knowing
> what is best for us."
>
> —Peter Marshall

Why do we sometimes get a no when we pray? The answers to that question will help you to understand that when God answers that way, it's because He has something far better for us than what we asked for. As Jesus said in Luke 11:11–12, "Which of you fathers, if your son asks for a fish, will give him a snake instead? Or if he asks for an egg, will give him a scorpion? If you then, though you are evil, know how to give good gifts to your children, how much more will your Father in heaven give the Holy Spirit to those who ask him!"

There are many examples in the Bible of God saying no to a prayer request, and the most important one to all of us is found in the Gospel of Luke, which records this prayer of Jesus: "Father, if you are willing, take this cup from me; yet not my will but yours be done." (Luke 22:42)

Jesus wasn't praying that His ultimate mission of providing salvation and forgiveness of sins be aborted. At that moment, Jesus was facing not just a cruel death on the Cross but temporary separation from the Father as He took on the sins of the world. His prayer was simply, "Father, is there any other way?"

God the Father answered Jesus and told Him no, and because Jesus was willing to accept that answer and obey His Father, all of us have the opportunity to inherit eternal life in heaven. When God said no, it was for His benefit, Jesus' benefit, and for our benefit.

The same is true for us when God says no.

✝ Faith in Action

When God tells us no, it's always for the best—the best for us, the best for those around us, and the best for His ultimate purposes for our lives.

Accept God's Loving Discipline

"God does not discipline us to subdue us, but to condition us for a life of usefulness and blessedness."
—Billy Graham

Many coaches who have made big names for themselves in the world of sports did so for one reason: discipline. The greats in their own games, such as Tom Landry and Vince Lombardi in professional football and John Wooden in college basketball, are known to have carved out hall of fame careers using discipline to shape the lives and games of the young men who played for them.

While the players who competed under these coaches probably wouldn't say that they enjoyed the kind of discipline they meted out, they would tell you that it had the desired results, namely that they were better players because of it.

The same principle rings true in the lives of those who have put their faith in a God who cared enough for them to send Jesus Christ to be their Savior.

Discipline is rarely a pleasant experience, but it is necessary if we are to be all we can be. In His infinite wisdom, God knows that His children need discipline. In fact, the Bible teaches that God's discipline is proof that we are His children in the first place. (See Hebrews 12:6.)

In *The Billy Graham Christian Worker's Handbook*, Graham explains that God's discipline is for our own good, because it: leads us to repentance, (2 Corinthians 7:9) restores us to fellowship with other believers, (1 John 1:3) makes us more faithful to Him, (1 Corinthians 4:2) humbles us, (2 Corinthians 12:7-9) teaches us spiritual discernment, (1 Corinthians 11:31, 32) and prepares us for service to His kingdom. (1 Corinthians 15:58)[6]

God doesn't expect any of us to enjoy it when He disciplines us, but He wants us to know, as many of our parents would have said, "This is for your own good."

✝ Faith in Action

When God disciplines us, it shows us two things. It shows us that He loves us and wants the very best for us and that He wants us to be ready and suitable for service to His kingdom.

✳Wait for God to Speak

> *"Behind the silence . . . are His higher thoughts.*
> *He is fitting stone to stone in His plan for the world*
> *and our lives, even though we can see only*
> *a confused and meaningless jumble of stones heaped*
> *together under a silent heaven."*
>
> —Helmut Thielicke

A poem found scrawled on a wall in a cellar where Jews had hidden from the Nazis during World War II contained the following words: I believe in God/even when he is silent.

We aren't usually comfortable with silence. When we speak to someone and hear nothing in return, we tend to believe there has been some kind of disconnect in our relationship or that the other person is angry or hurt and is giving us the silent treatment.

Sometimes when we don't hear from God, it's because for some reason our "spiritual ears" are keeping us from hearing His voice. In that case, it's time for us to do the things to open our ears to Him again. But there are also times when God, for reasons we can't immediately understand, keeps silent.

It's probably safe to say that every Christian has at some point in his or her life cried out to God asking a simple question or desperately for answers to some life crisis, only to hear silence. These can be frustrating times of wondering what we've done to make God so angry that He wouldn't speak to us, or wondering if our words of prayer didn't make it past our homes' ceilings.

There are three ways we can respond when God seems silent. The first is to become frustrated, angry, and cynical because we're not getting the answers we want when we want them. The second is to do the things necessary to unplug our ears so that we can again hear Him clearly. The third is to choose to continue walking in faith, knowing that even when we can't hear God or sense His presence, He's still there, working on our behalf simply because we have persevered.

✝ Faith in Action

There are times when we want to hear God only to hear silence. It is during those times when we need to wait for Him to speak.

Be Patient with Others

". . . God is a God of the second chance. Learn from
One who is patient with you, and you'll learn to be
patient with others."

—Woodrow Kroll

Abraham, the father of the nation of Israel, was sitting outside his tent when he saw an old man approaching. The man was weary from his journey, and Abraham rushed out to invite him into his tent. Abraham washed the old man's feet and gave him food and drink. Abraham noticed that the old man began eating and drinking—without saying a prayer.

"Don't you worship God?" Abraham asked.

"I worship fire only and reverence no other god," the old traveler replied.

Abraham was incensed when he heard this, and he grabbed the old man by the shoulders and threw him out.

Once he had departed, God called to Abraham and asked where the stranger had gone. Abraham replied, "I forced him out because he did not worship you."

God answered, "I have suffered him these eighty years. Could you not endure him one night?"

God's demonstrates His love for humankind in an endless number of ways, and one of those ways is His incredible (though not limitless) patience. While we as humans are very limited in our patience, God has demonstrated His patience throughout history.

Sadly, many people see God not as an infinitely loving and deeply patient Father but as some kind of celestial taskmaster ready to pounce on us the minute we step out of line. That misperception limits people in their relationship with God because they see Him as impossible to please. It also damages their relationships with others, because they tend to demonstrate the same kind of impatience with people that they believe God displays for them as individuals.

✝ Faith in Action

God is patient with humankind because He wants each and every person to have a chance to come to know Him, patient with the body of Christ as a whole because He wants it to be a perfect picture of Jesus, and patient with us as individuals because He desires more than anything that we become conformed to the image of His Son. (See Romans 8:29.)

Be Patient with God

"Circumstances may appear to wreck our lives and God's plans, but God is not helpless among the ruins. God's love is still working. He comes in and takes the calamity and uses it victoriously, working out His wonderful plan of love."

—Eric Liddell

Have you ever been in a situation where you feel like you're twisting in the wind, waiting for God to act on your behalf? Waiting for that job you feel is perfect for you? Waiting for God to change the heart of a wayward son or daughter? Waiting for the Lord to move at your request in bringing that friend or family member you've been praying for to come to a personal knowledge of Jesus Christ?

It's easy to fall into the "I want it, and I want it now" mode of thinking when it comes to asking God to move on our behalf. Our culture is one that values instant gratification. We want things done right away and are prone to becoming impatient and even frustrated when what we want doesn't happen *when* we want it to happen.

The psalmist David wrote of this kind of patience in waiting: "Be still before the Lord and wait patiently for him; do not fret when men succeed in their ways, when they carry out their wicked schemes. Refrain from anger and turn from wrath; do not fret—it leads only to evil." (Psalm 37:7–8)

The impatience and anger David warns us to avoid comes when we take our eyes off the fact that we serve a God who has never failed us and never will.

✝ Faith in Action

When we fall into "I want it now" thinking, it can become easy to start thinking that God isn't paying attention to you, that your needs, desires, and requests aren't important to Him. But nothing could be further from the truth. Our God is a loving heavenly Father who is concerned about the needs and desires of His children. However, He is also a God who wants us to be patient, knowing that sometimes He moves on our behalf in the nick of time and not a moment sooner.

Part 6

Trust

Depend on God

*"The best place any Christian can ever be
in is to be totally destitute and totally dependent
upon God, and know it."*

—Alan Redpath

James Hudson Taylor (1832–1905) was a man who knew firsthand about the absolute and complete dependability of God. Taylor was an English missionary who spent fifty-one years in China, where he founded the China Inland Mission, which, during his time of ministry, established twenty mission stations with 849 missionaries and trained around 700 Chinese missionaries. During that same time, China Inland Mission raised some $4 million and developed an active Chinese church of more than 125,000. Taylor himself is said to have won at least 35,000 converts and baptized 5,000.

Taylor was able to do all these things because he learned to depend on God to provide a way. He wrote in his personal journal of God's faithfulness and dependability: "Our heavenly Father is a very experienced One. He knows very well that

His children wake up with a good appetite every morning . . . He sustained three million Israelites in the wilderness for forty years. . . . Depend on it, God's work done in God's way will never lack God's supply." Jesus told His disciples that they must be dependent on Him for everything: "I am the vine; you are the branches. If a man remains in me and I in him, he will bear much fruit; apart from me you can do nothing." (John 15:5) He also demonstrated it in His dependence on God the Father: "I tell you the truth, the Son can do nothing by himself; he can do only what he sees his Father doing, because whatever the Father does the Son also does." (John 5:19)

Being a Christian means taking God at His word and believing that we can depend on Him for everything.

✝ Faith in Action

There is nothing God desires more in the life of the Christian than to have us completely dependent upon Him for everything we need to live a life of faith and to do the things He calls us to do.

Join God's Family

"You aren't loved because you're valuable.
You're valuable because God loves you."

—Anonymous

Jamie and Timmy grew up as brothers in the same home. If you were to meet the two boys, you would notice similarities in how they walked, how they talked, and even how they laughed.

When it comes to physical appearances, Timmy doesn't resemble either of his parents in how he looked. You see, Timmy was adopted when he was just a baby. He grew up enjoying the same kind of love and acceptance Jamie enjoyed in the security of his parents' home, even though the two are not biological brothers.

Just about every culture the world has ever known values adoption. It is a means by which God provides fathers for the fatherless and mothers for the motherless. And what makes adoption as a means of parenthood all the more blessed is that the parents choose to be mom and dad to a child who is not theirs—at least not in the biological sense.

Over and over, the Bible describes our relationship with God as being like that of a Father and His child. And the apostle Paul took that a step further when he wrote of that father-child relationship using the word adoption: "Because you are sons, God sent the Spirit of his Son into our hearts, the Spirit who calls out, 'Abba, Father.' So you are no longer a slave, but a son; and since you are a son, God has made you also an heir." (Galatians 4:6–7, italics added)

In this context, the word *Abba* is one not just of familiarity but of loving closeness. In today's culture, a fitting comparison to this word would be "Daddy." This tells us that God isn't just our Creator and Provider, but a heavenly Father who wants to have a close, loving relationship with His children.

What's even more wonderful about this is that God *chose* to be our Father.

✝ Faith in Action

Each of us was lost and fatherless—at least in the spiritual sense—but God chose to send His Son into the world to die so that we could become the children of God.

✸Know That God Loves You

> *"The Christian does not think God will love us because*
> *we are good, but that God will make us good because*
> *He loves us; just as the roof of a sun house does not*
> *attract the sun because it is bright, but becomes bright*
> *because the sun shines on it."*
>
> —C. S. Lewis

In the classic Christmastime cartoon *A Charlie Brown Christmas*, young Charlie goes outside to check his mailbox to see if he's received any Christmas cards. When he finds nothing, he sadly says, "I know nobody likes me. Why do we have to have a holiday season to emphasize it?"

The Bible has been referred to as God's love letter to the world. Indeed, God's Word is filled cover to cover with His expression of love—in His words as well as in His actions—for us.

God loves each of us . . .

- . . . *greatly*: "But God is so rich in mercy, and he loved us so very much. . . . " (Ephesians 2:4)
- . . . *ceaselessly*: "I have loved you with an everlasting love." (Jeremiah 31:3)
- . . . *unfailingly*: "Can a mother forget the baby at her breast and have no compassion on the child she has borne? Though she may forget, I will not forget you!" (Isaiah 49:15)
- . . . *with great delight*: "He will take great delight in you, he will quiet you with his love, he will rejoice over you with singing." (Zephaniah 3:17)
- . . . *sacrificially*: " . . . Christ loved us and gave himself up for us as a fragrant offering and sacrifice to God." (Ephesians 5:2)
- . . . *no matter what*: " . . . neither height nor depth, nor anything else in all creation, will be able to separate us from the love of God that is in Christ Jesus our Lord." (Romans 8:39)

✝ Faith in Action

During certain times in our lives, it's easy to believe that we're not loved. But there is one great source of love in which any of us can find comfort and fulfillment at any time: God.

Trust in God's Wisdom

> "As we trust God to give us wisdom for today's
> decisions, He will lead us a step at a time into what
> He wants us to be doing in the future."
>
> —Theodore Epp

Henry Ford, the founder of Ford Motor Company, was well known not just for his entrepreneurial spirit but also for his frugality.

One day, the generators at the Ford plant ground to a halt, paralyzing production. When the repairmen couldn't figure out the problem, Ford called Charlie Steinmetz, the man who built the generators, and asked him to help. Steinmetz tinkered with the generators for a few hours, then threw the switch. The generators whirred back to life.

Steinmetz sent Ford a bill for $10,000. Ford was stunned at the high price for the repairs and asked what exactly he was paying for. Steinmetz replied, "For tinkering with the generators, $10. For knowing where to tinker, $9,990."

We live in a world that still puts a high premium on wisdom, which we can define as not only knowing what to say, but also what to do, when to do it, how to do it, and why it's being done.

That's just the kind of wisdom our heavenly Father possesses. The Bible tells us that perfect, complete, and infinite wisdom is one of His many attributes. The prophet Jeremiah wrote that God has demonstrated this kind of wisdom to us from the beginning of creation: "He made the earth by his power; he founded the world by his wisdom and stretched out the heavens by his understanding." (Jeremiah 51:15)

Paul explained it this way: "I keep asking that the God of our Lord Jesus Christ, the glorious Father, may give you the Spirit of wisdom and revelation, so that you may know him better." (Ephesians 1:17)

✝ Faith in Action

Knowing that God has that kind of wisdom should be a great comfort to all Christians, no matter what their life situations look like. And it should also be comforting to know that God desires that we possess His wisdom and that He will give it to us generously if we do one thing: Ask in faith.

The Fatherhood of God

> *"Children do not find it difficult or complicated*
> *to talk to their parents, nor do they feel embarrassed*
> *to bring the simplest need to their attention.*
> *Neither should we hesitate to bring the simplest*
> *requests confidently to the Father."*
>
> —Richard J. Foster

There's a story about a Spanish boy who ran away from home after a falling out with his father. For months the father searched for his son but couldn't find him. As a last resort, he placed this ad in a Madrid newspaper: "Dear Paco, meet me in front of this newspaper office at noon on Saturday. All is forgiven. I love you. Your Father." That Saturday, the father showed up at the newspaper office at noon, where 800 boys named Paco waited, hoping to find the love and forgiveness offered in the newspaper ad.[7]

There is something inside of all of us that yearns for the kind of love and forgiveness only a father can give. But that is exactly the love God extended to all of us when He sent His Son, Jesus Christ, on an earthly mission to bring us back to Himself.

One thing Christians often overlook is that Christianity is not just a relationship, but a relationship between us and a loving heavenly Father. The apostle Paul wrote this of our Father/child relationship with God: "For you did not receive a spirit that makes you a slave again to fear, but you received the Spirit of sonship. And by him we cry, '*Abba*, Father.' The Spirit himself testifies that we are God's children." (Romans 8:15–16, italics added)

The apostle John wrote that God's motivation in calling us His children is love: "How great is the love the Father has lavished on us, that we should be called children of God! And that is what we are! The reason the world does not know us is that it did not know him." (1 John 3:1)

☩ Faith in Action

Our God isn't just a disinterested Creator but One who has chosen to be our heavenly Father, One who loves us far beyond our ability to comprehend.

Part 7

Prayer

In God's Presence

"Thou hast made us for thyself, O Lord, and our hearts are restless until they find their rest in thee."
—Augustine of Hippo

It has been said that the fear of the Lord can be partially defined as the fear of being away from the comfort, security, and affection of His presence for so much as a moment. While fearing God means a lot more than that, there is something to be said for maintaining a healthy fear of doing anything that would even temporarily take us out of God's presence.

The Old Testament prophet Isaiah wrote, "O Lord, be gracious to us; we long for you. Be our strength every morning, our salvation in time of distress." (Isaiah 33:2) Notice that Isaiah didn't say, "We long for your provision," or, "We long for your protection." His prayer was simply, "We long for *you*." He went on ask God to be the people's strength "every morning" and their salvation "in time of distress," meaning that we are to continually seek to walk in

God's presence—in good times as well as in difficult times.

The Psalms tell us that God's presence is a place of blessing and joy: "You will make known to me the path of life; In Your presence is fullness of joy; In Your right hand there are pleasures forever." (Psalm 16:11 New American Standard Bible) King David also wrote, "Blessed are those who have learned to acclaim you, who walk in the light of your presence, O Lord." (Psalm 89:15)

God doesn't call us just to say a prayer for salvation then begin following a set of rules. No, our calling from God is more personal and intimate than that.

✝ Faith in Action

God wants each of us to know Him as our Protector, Provider, loving Father, and faithful Friend. And once we've come to Him, we are never to walk away, even for a moment, but we are to do the things it takes to remain as close to Him as He desires to be to us.

Ask the Holy Spirit to Intercede

"Prayer has mighty power to move mountains because the Holy Spirit is ready both to encourage our praying and to remove the mountains hindering us. Prayer has the power to change mountains into highways."

—Wesley L. Duewel

In 1517, insurgents started a violent uprising in London, resulting in the arrests of hundreds of men, 300 of whom were quickly tried and hanged. Another 500 were thrown into prison, where they awaited their fates. As King Henry VIII sat on his throne, these men, each with ropes around their necks, were brought before the king. But before the king could sentence the men to death, three queens entered his quarters—Catharine of Aragon, wife of the king; Margaret, queen of Scotland, sister of the king; and Mary, queen of France, the king's other sister. The queens knelt before the throne and begged the king to spare the 500 men. The women remained at the king's feet until he forgave each and every one of them.[8]

This true-life story illustrates what the Bible calls intercession, which means "standing in the gap" on behalf of another person in prayer. But what happens when we ourselves struggle with what to pray and how to pray it? The Bible tells us that God Himself steps in and intercedes on our behalf. (See Romans 8:26–26.) Every believer will encounter situations where they don't quite know what to pray. We know God is concerned about what's going on in our lives, but what we don't know for sure is what He wants us to ask Him for. When that happens, we have an intercessor who has taken up residence inside us, who intimately knows our needs and desires, and who is ready to go before the Father on our behalf.

How exactly the Holy Spirit intercedes for us in response to our wordless groans has been a matter of debate for centuries. What we can know for certain, however, is that He is more than ready to be our Intercessor when we don't know what to pray for and ready to pray on our behalf according to the perfect will of God.

⁞ Faith in Action

When you don't know what or how to pray, ask the Holy Spirit to stand in the gap for you.

* Giving Ear to God's Gentle Whisper

"The value of consistent prayer is not that He will hear us, but that we will hear Him."

—William McGill

A high school teacher struggled with keeping the attention of some students in a particularly unruly afternoon history class. It seemed that the louder the teacher talked, the more disruptions broke out in the classroom. Even sending the "problem" students to the principal's office didn't help.

Finally, the beleaguered teacher remembered something his father had done when he wanted his attention. Rather than raise his voice, he would begin speaking slowly, quietly, and clearly. The teacher remembered how as a young boy, he knew that when his father spoke that way, it meant he needed to pay close attention.

The teacher had tried everything else, so he knew he had nothing to lose and tried the same thing with his students. Before long, he began to notice that when he spoke in a softer voice, his students began listening—sometimes leaning forward in their chairs and straining to hear what he had to say.

Sometimes when we pray and ask God to speak to us, we expect the skies to open up and a booming voice to come forward telling us what to do next. But as a loving and infinitely wise heavenly Father, God knows that we sometimes pay closer attention if He speaks softly and quietly—in what the Bible refers to as "a gentle whisper." (1 Kings 19:12)

God called the prophet Elijah for a meeting on a mountain. As Elijah waited, he saw winds so powerful that he thought they might tear the mountain apart, a powerful earthquake, and a huge fire. But God didn't speak to Elijah through any of those things but spoke to him in a soft, gentle voice, asking him first, "What are you doing here, Elijah?" (1 Kings 19:13) In the end, Elijah received just the answers he had sought.

✝ Faith in Action

If you need answers from God, pay close attention to the gentle whispers God may be sending your way. It's very often the way He knows will get your attention.

✳ Read the Bible . . . Again

> *"No man is uneducated who knows the Bible, and no one is wise who is ignorant of its teachings."*
> —Samuel Chadwick

Who among us hasn't started setting up that new computer, DVD player, or home stereo, only to throw up our hands in frustration when we can't quite figure out how to make the thing function as it was designed? Sometimes it seems that the front cover of these items' owners manuals should contain this little bit of wisdom: "When all else fails, read the instructions."

Sadly, many believers fail to read the instructions God has provided us for living a victorious, vigorous life of faith. Those instructions are found in the pages of the bestselling book of all time, the Bible.

When we Christians fail to regularly read and constantly heed the instructions recorded in God's Word, we are sure to find ourselves frustrated and disillusioned. On the other hand, those of us who make reading, studying, meditating on, and applying what

God has told us in the Bible will enjoy lives of growing faith and victory.

A well-known but anonymously written piece of wisdom, partially reprinted here, shows us why we should make the Bible central in our lives of faith:

> This book contains the mind of God, the state of man, the way of salvation, the doom of sinners, and the happiness of believers.
>
> Its doctrines are holy, its precepts are binding, its histories are true, and its decisions are immutable.

Martin Luther, whose words and actions started what historians call the Protestant Reformation, described his method of Bible study this way: "I study my Bible as I gather apples. First, I shake the whole tree that the ripest might fall. Then I shake each limb, and when I have shaken each limb, I shake each branch and every twig. Then I look under every leaf."

✝ Faith in Action

It's not enough to simply read the Bible. We must study it, meditate on it, pray over it, and make it a part of our very being. We must treat it as the absolutely essential instruction book for every part of our lives.

Tap into the Power of the Holy Spirit

"God's power under us, in us, surging through us, is exactly what turns dependence into unforgettable experiences of completeness."

—Bruce Wilkinson

A woman knew that her car was running low on gasoline, but this was a particularly busy day, with five or six errands to run. After each stop, she told herself, "I can make one more errand."

Finally, the woman had run one errand too many. When she turned the key, her car wouldn't start because it had run out of fuel.

Just as the woman's car couldn't operate without gasoline, we as Christians can't live the way God wants us to without the empowerment of the Holy Spirit. The Bible tells us that the Holy Spirit is our source of power for living the Christian life, but it also tells us that the Holy Spirit is not simply a power source but a person—just as God the Father and God the Son are persons.

A. W. Tozer, the twentieth-century preacher and writer, said this of the person of the Holy Spirit: ". . . the Holy Spirit is not the personification of anything. . . . He has individuality. . . . He can hear, speak, desire, grieve, and rejoice. He is a Person."

Jesus told His disciples, "But the Helper, the Holy Spirit, *whom* the Father will send in My name, *He* will teach you all things, and bring to your remembrance all that I said to you." (John 14:26 New American Standard Bible, italics added)

As our Helper and Teacher, the Holy Spirit works to reveal to us the things of God, (1 Corinthians 2:10, 13) reveals the things of Jesus Christ, (John 16:14) reminds us of Jesus' words, (John 14:26) directs us in living godly lives, (Isaiah 30:21) and guides us into truth. (John 16:13)

✝ Faith in Action

Since the Holy Spirit is a person, He can be grieved, (Ephesians 4:30) angered, (Isaiah 63:10) and resisted. (Acts 7:51) But He can also be obeyed (read Acts 10:19–21 for an example) and can dwell within us, (John 14:17) both of which give us the power to do great things for God and the guarantee of receiving God's greatest blessings.

Part 8

Comfort

Take Comfort from a Heavenly Friend

"Our valleys may be filled with foes and tears; but we can lift our eyes to the hills to see God and the angels, heaven's spectators, who support us according to God's infinite wisdom as they prepare our welcome home."

—Billy Graham

Joseph Scriven was born in 1819 with the proverbial silver spoon in his mouth. He grew up in his native Ireland with a wealthy and devoted and loving family. Later, he met the woman who was the love of his life, and they made plans to marry. On the eve of his wedding, tragedy struck. His fiancée drowned, sending him into a long bout of grief and depression.

Not long after his fiancée's death, Scriven left his homeland and moved to Port Hope, Canada, where he began devoting his time to being a friend, comforter, and helper to those around him.

Later, Scriven received word that his mother had fallen seriously ill. Scriven wrote her a letter of comfort that reflected what he found out as he suffered through the pain and sorrow of losing his beloved, namely that the one place he could always turn for comfort was to the best Friend he would ever have, Jesus Christ.

Scriven's life following his tragedy reflected what the apostle Paul wrote about how God comforts us and how He desires that we be a comfort to others: "Praise be to the God and Father of our Lord Jesus Christ, the Father of compassion and the God of all comfort, who comforts us in all our troubles, so that we can comfort those in any trouble with the comfort we ourselves have received from God." (2 Corinthians 1:3)

✛ Faith in Action

God cares for each of us with a deep, everlasting love and compassion. When we are hurting, when we can't understand why life is treating us the way it is, we have a Source of heavenly comfort. He's not just our Creator and provider; He's our loving heavenly Father, and He cares deeply when we are hurting and wants to hold us in His comforting arms.

There's No Place God Is Not

"God is so big He can cover the whole world with Love and so small He can curl up inside your heart."

—Anonymous

There's an old poem about a young boy on his way home from Sunday school who stopped to enjoy some of the everyday examples of God's creation. He observed a little caterpillar, which he knew would somehow miraculously become a beautiful butterfly. He saw a bird's nest hanging in a tree overhead, and he marveled at how the mother bird so carefully constructed the nest.

As the boy made his way home, his neighbor asked him where he'd been that morning. "I've been to Sunday school," the young boy eagerly said. "And I've learned a lot about God!"

"I'll tell you what," the neighbor said. "If you can tell me where God is, I'll give you a dime."

The boy wasted no time answering, for he had seen the evidence of God all around him that morning: "I'll give you a dollar, Mister, if you tell me where God ain't!"

There truly is no place that God is not. Speaking through the Old Testament prophet Jeremiah, He tells us, "'Can anyone hide in secret places so that I cannot see him?' declares the Lord. 'Do not I fill heaven and earth?'" (Jeremiah 23:24)

While some people aren't totally comfortable with the idea that God sees them at all times, King David's words of praise for his God gave His people comfort: "Where can I go from your Spirit? Where can I flee from your presence? If I go up to the heavens, you are there; if I make my bed in the depths, you are there. If I rise on the wings of the dawn, if I settle on the far side of the sea, even there your hand will guide me, your right hand will hold me fast." (Psalm 139:7–10)

✝ Faith in Action

No matter where you are, you can be assured that God is there for you. Knowing that, you can be assured that He is but one word of prayer away when you have questions, needs, or a desire to simply enjoy His presence.

Made in His Image, But Why?

"You have to live with Him day by day, and year by year, and to learn to know Him as we learn to know husbands and wives, by continual experience of a sweet and unfailing love, by many a sacred hour of interchange of affection and reception of gifts and counsels."

—Alexander MacLaren

The Bible tells us over and over that God is a God of love and that He wants more than anything for us miserable little humans to respond to Him in kind. In short, He wants a personal, loving relationship with each of us as individuals. That is why when God created us humans, out of all the creatures He made, He gave us and us alone the capacity to respond to Him in love and obedience.

That is partly what the Bible means when it says, "So God created man in his own image, in the image of God he created him; male and female he created them." (Genesis 1:27) We are the only beings God speaks to, gives commandments to, shares His love personally with, and gives Himself to.

The framers of the Westminster Shorter Catechism, which was a series of questions compiled in 1647 by a group of Scottish and English clergy, started their document by posing and answering the question of why we are here in the first place:

- Question 1: What is the chief end [or destiny] of man?
- Answer 1: Man's chief end is to glorify God, and to enjoy Him for ever.

When God created humankind, He designed us to be like Him in many ways but with obvious limitations. We wouldn't be all-knowing or all-powerful like He is, and we wouldn't have the power to create like He does.

What we *would* be able to do is have a personal relationship with Him. God wasn't interested in creating a bunch of mindless, emotionless robots. His love required that He created us with minds, souls, and spirits—all of which we have the privilege of submitting to Him so that we could enjoy His love . . . now and for all of eternity.

✝ Faith in Action

We were made in God's image so that we could respond to His love by loving Him in return.

Take Comfort in Your Never-Changing God

"Our circumstances are not an accurate reflection of God's goodness. Whether life is good or bad, God's goodness, rooted in His character, is the same."

—Helen Grace Lescheid

When twentieth-century novelist Lloyd C. Douglas was a university student, he lived in a boarding house, one floor up from an elderly, retired music teacher who was unable to leave his apartment. Douglas and the man had a daily morning ritual. Douglas would go down the steps, open the old man's door, and ask, "Well, what's the good news?" The old man would pick up his tuning fork, tap it on the side of his wheelchair and say, "That's middle C! It was middle C yesterday; it will be middle C tomorrow; it will be middle C a thousand years from now!"

There's great comfort in knowing we can always count on something or someone, in knowing that there are constants in our lives. For the believer, we can always count on God, and the reason we can depend on Him is this: God never has to adapt to anything, and because He is perfect in all His ways, He's never had to change.

The Bible teaches very clearly that God has never changed and will never change. Theologians call this personal attribute of God His immutability. While *we* change and our life circumstances change, we can always count on God to be not just the Creator but our loving heavenly Father.

The apostle James wrote that God has made the decision to bring us into His kingdom, and that this decision is irrevocable: "Every good and perfect gift is from above, coming down from the Father of the heavenly lights, who does not change like shifting shadows. He chose to give us birth through the word of truth, that we might be a kind of first fruits of all he created." (James 1:17–18)

✝ Faith in Action

Our world will change, our friends and family will change, and we ourselves will change. But God will never change, and we can always count on Him to keep each and every one of His promises.

Look to God for Restoration

"God sees with utter clarity who we are. He is unde-ceived as to our warts and wickedness. But when God looks at us that is not all He sees. He also sees who we are intended to be, who we will one day become."

—John Ortberg

Several years ago, a man seriously vandalized Rembrandt's famous painting, *"The Night Watch."* Museum officials were faced with the need to spend whatever it would take to restore it. They hired the best art experts money could buy, and they worked painstakingly to restore the damaged treasure.

God does the same thing with His people when they fall into sin or when they go through "dry times" in their walk with Him. He loves and values His children too much to give up on us. So rather than just tossing us aside and giving up on us, He does every-thing necessary to restore us to Himself.

The Old Testament prophet Joel records God's promise to restore and redeem the time His people spent in rebellion against Him: "I will repay you for the years the locusts have eaten—the great locust and the young locust, the other locusts and the locust swarm—my great army that I sent among you. You will have plenty to eat, until you are full, and you will praise the name of the Lord your God, who has worked wonders for you; never again will my people be shamed. Then you will know that I am in Israel, that I am the Lord your God, and that there is no other; never again will my people be shamed." (Joel 2:25–27)

Each of us will go through difficult times in our lives—some of them because of our own waywardness and some through no fault of our own.

✟ Faith in Action

God wants each of us to understand that He wants to restore us when we fall or when our lives seem dry and barren. He is our loving heavenly Father, and He wants not just to walk with us during the difficult times but to restore what we may have lost during those times.

Part 9

Faith

Leave the Worrying to God

*"Be not miserable about what may happen tomorrow.
The same everlasting Father, who cares for you today,
will care for you tomorrow."*

—St. Francis de Sales

We're all familiar with the term "worried sick."
Perhaps you know someone who has allowed
himself or herself to be so consumed with worry that
he or she actually felt ill. There can be consequences
for the "stress monster" worse than the general misery
and mental stress we feel when we worry too much.
Excessive anxiety or worry can lead to actual physical
conditions.

There is an endless list of things we can choose
to worry about in today's world. Family concerns,
financial needs, and personal conflicts are but a few
of the things that can drive us to worry.

But God never intended for us to be held captive by worry over any of these things. Over and over
God's Word tells us that we needn't worry, because
He's aware of all our needs and is working on our
behalf to meet them.

Probably the best-known Scripture passage on the subject of worry is found in the Gospel of Matthew, which contains the famous Sermon on the Mount. In it, Jesus addressed our all-too-human tendencies to worry when He said, "Therefore I tell you, do not worry about your life, what you will eat or drink; or about your body, what you will wear. Is not life more important than food, and the body more important than clothes?" (6:24–26)

In short, when it comes to worry, Jesus says one thing: don't.

The apostle Paul, enlarging a bit on the words of Jesus, gave us a practical way to deal with our worries: "Do not be anxious about anything, but in everything, by prayer and petition, with thanksgiving, present your requests to God." (Philippians 4:6)

✝ Faith in Action

God leaves many choices up to us, and one of them is this: Will we allow ourselves to become so consumed with worry that we make ourselves miserable, even sick, or will we take our needs, concerns, and problems to a God who wants to hear from us and who wants to give us His perfect peace?

Express Your Doubts

"Many Christians believe in what Christ did for them in the past and will do for them in the future. But they do not believe He can do anything for them now."

—Zig Ziglar

G. Campbell Morgan had already enjoyed success as a preacher by the time he was nineteen years old, but around that time he began to have doubts about the Bible. The writings of scientists and agnostics caused him to question what he had always believed in.

Morgan had to know if what he had believed in and preached on was the truth so he purchased a new Bible. He said to himself, "If it be the Word of God, and if I come to it with an unprejudiced and open mind, it will bring assurance to my soul of itself." With doubts still haunting him, Morgan began reading his new Bible. The result was that he became more convinced than ever that God was everything the Bible tells us He is.[9]

The Bible tells us that we are to have faith in God and in His promises, but how should we handle our doubts when they arise? The first thing we need to do is realize that God won't be offended if we bring our doubts to Him.

The Bible tells the story of a man who had some doubts about Jesus' power to heal his demon-possessed son. When the man came to Jesus, he asked Him to help his son—*if* He could. Jesus replied, "'If you can?' Everything is possible for him who believes." (Mark 9:23)

The boy's father immediately exclaimed: "I do believe; help me overcome my unbelief!" (Mark 9:24) Rather than send the man away, Jesus responded to what faith he had and to his honesty and cast the demon out of his son.

✝ Faith in Action

When we are honest with God about our doubts, when we tell Him, "I do believe; help me overcome my unbelief!" He shows us that we can trust Him in every area of our lives.

Dwell in the Future

"Every tomorrow has two handles. We can take hold of it by the handle of anxiety, or by the handle of faith."
—Henry Ward Beecher

Instead of looking forward to the great things God wants to do in the here and now and in the future, many believers insist on looking backward—at their past failures and successes in their walks with God. Some are frozen by the fear that they will fail the way they had before, and others tend to rest on their laurels, but God's Word tells us that we are to focus on what's going on in our lives right now.

The apostle Paul wrote, "Brothers, I do not consider myself yet to have taken hold of it. But one thing I do: Forgetting what is behind and straining toward what is ahead, I press on toward the goal to win the prize for which God has called me heavenward in Christ Jesus." (Philippians 3:13–14) In other words, don't live in the past but instead live for God in the present and in the future, knowing that He is firmly in control of both.

In a sermon delivered on January 2, 1887, the great preacher Charles Haddon Spurgeon said, "The God of the past has blotted out your sin, the God of the present makes all things work for your good, the God of the future will never leave you nor forsake you."

The sins and mistakes we have committed in the past are buried in a sea of forgetfulness, never to be remembered. We are to leave things that we have done for the Lord behind, knowing that God will remember them when the time comes for us to receive our eternal reward.

The Bible gives only one reason to look back at the past, and that's to remember the great things that God has done for us.

✝ Faith in Action

In the Old Testament, passage after passage admonishes the people of Israel to remember the great and miraculous things God had done for His people. The application for us today is to remember what He has done in the past, but with an eye open for the present and the future.

God's Guidance

"The beautiful thing about this adventure called faith is that we can count on Him never to lead us astray."

—Charles R. Swindoll

It's safe to say that most Christians at some point in their walks with the Lord have struggled with the question of how they can know God will provide for their own lives. However, this may be the wrong question to ask.

King Solomon, the writer of most of the Book of Proverbs wrote: "Trust in the Lord with all your heart, and lean not on your own understanding; In all your ways acknowledge Him, and He shall direct your paths." (Proverbs 3:5-6) In other words, instead of simply asking what God wants us to do, we should focus on knowing and trusting Him better, trusting that He will lead us where He wants to go and when He wants us to go there.

Elisabeth Elliot, who served as a missionary for many years in the jungles of Ecuador, illustrated our need for God's guidance when she wrote, "What we really ought to have is the Guide himself."[10] Jesus likened our relationship with Him with that of sheep to the shepherd when He said, " . . . the sheep hear his voice; and he calls his own sheep by name and leads them out. And when he brings out his own sheep, he goes before them; and the sheep follow him, for they know his voice." (John 10:3–4)

The disciples didn't usually ask Jesus what was on the agenda for a given day. Instead, they simply followed Him wherever He led and did whatever He said to do. The results? They became the instruments God used to start His church and reach people all over the world with the message of the Gospel of Jesus Christ.

✝ Faith in Action

Seek the person of God first, and He'll give you the guidance you want and need.

The Names of Jesus

*"There are two hundred and fifty-six names given
in the Bible for the Lord Jesus Christ, and I suppose
this was because He was infinitely beyond all
that any one name could express."*

—Billy Sunday

The Bible is filled cover to cover with different names for Jesus, and each tells us something about Jesus' character, mission, and promises. The Lord Jesus Christ is:

- ... *The Author of Life* (Acts 3:15) because He is the only way to an eternity in heaven.
- ... *The Bread of God* (John 6:33) because He is God's provision for our salvation.
- ... *Good Shepherd* (John 10:11, 14) because He leads us daily.
- ... *Wonderful Counselor* (Isaiah 9:6) because we can trust Him as we struggle through day-to-day life.
- ... *The Deliverer* (Romans 11:26) because He has released us from the power of Satan and sin.

- ... *The Son of God* (John 1:49) and the *Son of Man* (Matthew 8:20) because He was 100 percent divine yet 100 percent human.
- ... *The Lamb without Blemish* (1 Peter 1:19) because He was tempted yet without sin.
- ... *The Lamb of God* (John 1:29) because He was God's once-and-for-all sacrifice for our sins.
- ... *The King Eternal* (1 Timothy 1:17) because He will reign forever.
- ... *The Light of the World* (John 8:12) because He shows us the way.
- ... *The Word of God* (Revelation 19:13) because He is God's message of love to a lost world.
- ... *Our Righteousness* (1 Corinthians 1:30) because when God sees us in all our imperfection, He sees the perfection of Jesus.
- ... *The Christ* (1 John 2:22) because He came to deliver us from the power of sin and death.
- ... *The Savior* (Ephesians 5:23) because without Him we would all be lost forever.

⁝ Faith in Action

When we know the names of Jesus in the Bible, we know we truly can count on Him to keep every one of His promises—promises for our salvation, for our forgiveness, and for life eternal with Him and our heavenly Father.

Part 10

Humility

The Fear of God: What It Means

> "Where there is fear of God to keep the house, the enemy can find no way to enter."
>
> —St. Francis of Assisi

In the classic C. S. Lewis novel *The Lion, the Witch and the Wardrobe*, there is a passage where two talking animals, Mr. and Mrs. Beaver, prepare two girls, Susan and Lucy, to meet Aslan the lion, who is an allegorical picture of Jesus.

When Mrs. Beaver informs the girls that Aslan is a lion, one of them becomes very nervous and asks if it's safe to be in his presence. Mr. Beaver responds by telling the girls that Aslan is not *safe*, but he is *good*.

This illustrates a theme, one that seems at a glance to be rather contradictory, that runs throughout the Bible, namely the fear of God.

In the Bible, we are commanded to fear God (Psalm 22:23, 1 Peter 2:17) and told that the fear of God is the beginning of wisdom (Psalm 111:10) and that it is of eternal value. (Psalm 19:9) At the same time God identifies Himself in His Word as a loving heavenly Father who has given everything He has in order that He may have an intimate, personal relationship with us.

When Lewis wrote of Jesus using the form of a lion, he is using a description that makes us think of a ferocious, dangerous animal. But at the same time, Aslan is different from a literal lion, because he is at the same time awesome and powerful yet good, gentle, and trustworthy.

✝ Faith in Action

Our God has identified Himself as One for whom we should have deep reverence and respect, but also someone in whom we can trust implicitly. As His children, our "fear" of Him isn't to be dread—as we would feel toward a lion—but one of absolute trust, knowing that He means us well in every way.

Recognizing God's Control

"I will charge my soul to believe and wait for Him,
and will follow His providence, and not go before it,
nor stay behind it."

—Samuel Rutherford

Consider for a moment the story of Joseph, one of the founding fathers of the nation of Israel.

At first, things went pretty well for Joseph in Egypt. He was a servant of a man named Potiphar, an officer of Pharaoh. In time, he rose to a trusted position in Potiphar's household. But that changed when Potiphar's wife falsely accused Joseph of attempted rape, a charge that landed him in prison.

Even though Joseph was the victim of a grave injustice, he remained faithful to God and to the purposes for which he had been called. Eventually, Joseph's faithfulness paid dividends, as a sequence of events gave him the opportunity to interpret the dreams of Pharaoh, and he became a trusted confidant of him.

It was from that position of respect and power that Joseph was able to keep Egypt from suffering through a terrible famine and to provide for his family. When Joseph finally confronted those who had sold him into slavery, he didn't curse them or vow revenge. Instead, he forgave them and said, "You intended to harm me, but God intended it for good to accomplish what is now being done, the saving of many lives." (Genesis 50:20)

God could just as easily have rescued Joseph from his brothers or from the hands of the men who delivered him to Potiphar. But He had a greater purpose in mind for Joseph and for his situation. For that reason, He left Joseph right where he was.

Theologians would call this an example of God's providence, but the apostle Paul put it in layman's terms when he wrote to the Roman church, "And we know that in *all things* God works for the good of those who love him, who have been called according to his purpose." (Romans 8:28, italics added)

✝ Faith in Action

In our own lives, this means that no matter what we are going through, God is working to bring something that is of benefit to us, to others, or to both.

Acknowledging God's Power

> "If God were small enough to be understood, He would
> not be big enough to be worshiped."
> —Evelyn Underhill

Many years ago, comedian George Carlin posed this rather loaded question: "Can God make a rock so big that He Himself cannot lift it?"

Cynics and pseudo-intellectuals have posed questions like that one throughout the course of human history, not in an attempt to gain information about God but to take verbal swipes at the attributes of God as listed in the Bible, namely His omnipotence.

Omnipotence is a theological-sounding word that simply means that God is all-powerful, able to do anything He wants to do any time He wants to do it. The Bible includes many declarations and examples of God's power.

There are Self-imposed limitations to what God can do, not because He lacks the power but because some things go against His nature. For example, the writer of the epistle to the Hebrews states, " . . . it is impossible for God to lie." (Hebrews 6:18)

What God's nature keeps Him from doing is nothing when compared to what He can and has done. It was because of His awesome power that God could, among many other things . . .

- . . . create the heavens and the earth out of nothing. (Genesis 2)
- . . . cause a barren old woman to give birth. (Genesis 18)
- . . . bring plagues upon the land of Egypt, forcing Pharaoh to release the children of Israel from slavery. (Exodus 8–11)
- . . . cause His own Son to be born of a virgin so that He could live and die sacrificially.
- . . . raise His crucified Son from the dead so that He could defeat death for us all.

✝ Faith in Action

Knowing that we serve a God of such power is both awe-inspiring and comforting. After all, if He can do all those things for you and me, we should have no trouble believing that He can step into our little worlds and make the kind of difference we need made.

Blessings in Obedience

"The man that believes will obey; failure to obey is convincing proof that there is no true faith present. To attempt the impossible God must give faith or there will be none, and He gives faith to the obedient heart only."

—A. W. Tozer

Hall of Fame quarterback Roger Staubach, who led the Dallas Cowboys to world championships in Super Bowls VI in 1972 and XII in 1978—earning the Most Valuable Player award in Super Bowl VI— played for the Cowboys under another Hall of Famer, coach Tom Landry.

While the two men enjoyed spectacular success together, playing for Landry was something of a trial for Staubach. In a time when most quarterbacks called their own plays, Landry sent in every play, giving Staubach specific instructions as to when he was to pass and when he was to run. Staubach was allowed to change the play only in emergency situations.

One thing Staubach couldn't argue with was the results. Later, he acknowledged that his relationship with Landry taught him a valuable lesson on the subject of obedience: "I faced up to the issue of obedience. Once I learned to obey, there was harmony, fulfillment, and victory."

The apostle Paul wrote of our response of obedience to God, "Your attitude should be the same as that of Christ Jesus: Who, being in very nature God, did not consider equality with God something to be grasped, but made himself nothing, taking the very nature of a servant, being made in human likeness. And being found in appearance as a man, he humbled himself and became obedient to death—even death on a cross!" (Philippians 2:5–8)

In our culture, the word *obedience* is not a popular one. However, even though times have changed, our God has not, and He not only demands our obedience to Himself and His Word, He has proven Himself more than worthy of it.

✝ Faith in Action

The Bible promises us blessing if we willfully and without reservation give ourselves to God in obedience. Jesus stated this very simply and directly when He said, "Blessed rather are those who hear the word of God and obey it." (Luke 11:28)

Respect the Ultimate Promise-Keeper

"Go to the Bible to meet Christ. . . . He is its author, its subject matter, the doorway to its treasures, the full-throated symphony of which Adam and the prophets heard just the faintest tune."

—Andre Seu

Charles Ryrie, a biblical scholar, teacher, and author of many Christian books, has pointed out that according to the laws of chance, it would take 200 billion earths populated with 4 billion people each for one person whose life would accurately fulfill 100 prophecies without any errors in sequence. What makes those figures all the more amazing, however, is that Jesus fulfilled more than 300 prophecies found in the Bible concerning His first coming.

In literally hundreds of Old Testament prophecies, the Bible pointed toward Jesus as the coming Messiah, then recorded how He fulfilled those prophecies. Here are just a few examples:

- He would be a descendant of King David (2 Samuel 7:16)—fulfilled in Matthew 1:1.
- He would demonstrate great compassion (Isaiah 42:3)—fulfilled in Matthew 11:4–5.
- He would declare that the Scriptures were written about Him (Psalm 40:6–8)—fulfilled in Luke 24:44.
- He would declare that He was the Son of God (Psalm 2:7)—fulfilled in John 9:35–37.
- He would perform miraculous healings (Isaiah 35:5–6)—fulfilled in many passages, including Mark 10:51–52, Mark 7:32–35, and Matthew 12:10–13.
- His feet and hands would be pierced (Psalm 22:16)—fulfilled in Matthew 27:38.
- He would die a violent death (Zechariah 13:7)—fulfilled in Matthew 27:35.
- He would be raised from the dead and live forever (Isaiah 53:10)—fulfilled in Mark 16:16.

✝ Faith in Action

When we read these and the many other Old Testament prophecies Jesus fulfilled, we can conclude that Jesus proved that He is everything He claimed to be and that God keeps all of His promises down to the last detail.

Part 11

Hope

✳ Where We Place Our Hope

*"He who breathes into our hearts the heavenly hope
will not deceive or fail us when we press forward to its
realization."*

—Anonymous

Thomas à Kempis, the fifteenth-century German monk who is credited with writing or editing *The Imitation of Christ*, one of the most widely read books on spirituality of all time, told this story of a man who learned what putting his hope in God really meant:

> One day when a certain man who wavered often and anxiously between hope and fear was struck with sadness, he knelt in humble prayer before the altar of a church. While meditating on these things, he said, "Oh if I but knew whether I should persevere to the end!" Instantly he heard within the divine answer: "If you knew this, what would you do? Do now what you would do then and you will be quite secure." Immediately consoled and comforted, he resigned himself to the divine will and the

anxious uncertainty ceased. His curiosity no longer sought to know what the future held for him, and he tried instead to find the perfect, the acceptable will of God in the beginning and end of every good work.

The Bible tells us repeatedly that we are going to put our hope in one place, and it's not in our own talents, not in our own abilities. We are to put our hope in God and God alone. And, as King David wrote, "No one whose hope is in you will ever be put to shame." (Psalm 25:3)

When we talk about the hope God gives us when we place our faith in Him, it's not in the same context as one who has a need but no faith saying something like, "I *hope* something good happens." Far from it. Placing our hope in God means we are hopeful because we know He's going to come through for us.

⊹ Faith in Action

We can place our hope and our confidence in God and in His promises, even in those times when we are suffering, when our circumstances may seem hopeless.

A God Who Affirms Us

"Our valleys may be filled with foes and tears; but we can lift our eyes to the hills to see God and the angels, heaven's spectators, who support us according to God's infinite wisdom as they prepare our welcome home."

—Billy Graham

At age sixteen, world-renowned pianist/conductor Andor Foldes had already become a skilled pianist but was troubled because of a personal conflict with his piano teacher.

In the midst of that very troubled year, Emil von Sauer, one of the most highly regarded pianists of the day, came to Budapest, where Foldes was living, to perform.

Sauer requested that Foldes play for him, and the young man obliged the master. When he finished, Sauer walked over to him, kissed him on the forehead, and said, "My son, when I was your age I became a student of Liszt. He kissed me on the forehead after my first lesson, saying, 'Take good care of this kiss—it comes from Beethoven, who gave it me after hearing me play.' I have waited for years to pass on this sacred heritage, but now I feel you deserve it."[11]

At some points in our lives, we all need to be affirmed and encouraged. And as children of God, we have an Affirmer who knows our every thought and action and who affirms us and reminds us constantly of His great love for us.

The Bible is filled with God's declarations of love, commitment, and encouragement for His people, one of the most beautiful of which is found in the writings of a relatively obscure prophet named Zephaniah: "The Lord your God is with you, he is mighty to save. He will take great delight in you, he will quiet you with his love, he will rejoice over you with singing." (Zephaniah 3:17)

✝ Faith in Action

When we are going through times of discouragement, we should seek our affirmation and encouragement from our heavenly Father, realizing that He gives those things freely to people who place their faith in Jesus Christ and endeavor to serve Him.

Part 12

Gratitude

✳ Give Thanks

"(The soul) must forget about (understanding) and abandon itself into the arms of love, and His Majesty will teach it what to do next; almost its whole work is to realize its unworthiness to receive such great good and to occupy itself in thanksgiving."

—Teresa of Avila

Alexander Whyte (1832–1921) was a Presbyterian minister in Scotland known for, among other things, some very memorable—and inspirational— prayers from the pulpit. Whyte never failed to give thanks, and he always included gratitude in his prayers before the congregation. One gloomy, stormy Sunday morning as Whyte arose to pray, someone in his congregation thought, Certainly the preacher won't think of anything for which to thank the Lord on a wretched day like this. This churchgoer, however, underestimated Whyte's capacity for gratefulness. Whyte began his prayer by praying, "We thank Thee, O God, that the weather is not always like this."

This attitude of gratitude is demonstrated over and over throughout the Bible, and probably nowhere more than in the book of Psalms, which was written by men who endured more than their share of adversity and persecution. In the Psalms we read of giving thanks for, among many other things, God's goodness, provision, love, and protection. Here are just a few examples:

- "The Lord is my strength and my shield; my heart trusts in him, and I am helped. My heart leaps for joy and I will give thanks to him in song." (Psalm 28:7)
- "Enter his gates with thanksgiving and his courts with praise; give thanks to him and praise his name." (Psalm 100:4)
- "Give thanks to the Lord, for he is good; his love endures forever." (Psalm 107:1)

✝ Faith in Action

What do we have to be thankful for? Start with the provision He's made for our salvation through His Son Jesus Christ. Then we can thank Him for giving us the privilege of being able to know Him intimately and communicate with Him freely. From there, we can express our gratitude for His provision for our physical needs. From there, we'll find no end of things for which to thank our heavenly Father.

The God We "Get to" Worship

*"Worship is the submission of all our nature
to God . . . the quickening of conscience by his
holiness, the nourishment of the mind with his truth,
the purifying of the imagination by his beauty,
the opening of the heart to his love, the surrender of
the will to his purpose."*

—William Temple

In the classic devotional *My Utmost for His Highest*,
Oswald Chambers defines worship as "giving God
the best that He has given you." In other words, our
worship and adoration for our heavenly Father should
come from hearts and lives He has blessed with the
very best He has to offer: Himself.

We should never see worship as something we
have to do but something we *get* to do. And we get to
do it simply because God has invited us to do so.

One unchangeable truth about God is that He
knows who He is, and He doesn't need our praise and
worship to affirm it. But God allows us to enjoy His
presence through our words and actions of praise for

Him. When we praise and worship God, we allow Him to share a good thing with us—the best thing there is.

God created human beings for one primary purpose: to praise and worship Him. And He didn't do that out of any sense of need, either. He did it because He wanted to create beings with whom He could share a mutual, eternal love. He wanted humans to willingly and joyfully praise Him from their hearts.

The Book of Psalms in many places reads like a "how to" and "why to" when it comes to praising God. In one of his Psalms, King David wrote these words of willful and joyous praise: "I will bow down toward your holy temple and will praise your name for your love and your faithfulness, for you have exalted above all things your name and your word." (Psalm 138:2)

✝ Faith in Action

We should never look at praising and worshiping God as something we *have* to do but something we *get* to do. And when we choose to make praise and worship a part of our everyday lives, God shares with us the very best He has: Himself!

Thank Heaven for Heaven

"But the best definition of it is to say that heaven is that state where we will always be with Jesus, and where nothing will separate us from Him anymore."

—William Barclay

The fourteenth chapter of the Gospel of John describes an emotional scene between Jesus and His disciples prior to His death. In this scene, Jesus tells them that He is going away, but that it was for their benefit that He did so, because He would be preparing a place for them . . . in heaven.

"In my Father's house are many rooms," Jesus told them, "if it were not so, I would have told you. I am going there to prepare a place for you. And if I go and prepare a place for you, I will come back and take you to be with me that you also may be where I am." (John 14:2–3)

Heaven, the place that Jesus called "paradise" (Luke 23:43), is the ultimate destination for all those who put their faith in Jesus Christ. The Bible tells us that we are all just visitors here on earth, that we have an eternal home waiting for us after we die.

This eternal home called heaven is . . .

- . . . created by God. (Genesis 1:1, Revelation 10:6)
- . . . eternal. (Psalm 88:29, 2 Corinthians 5:1)
- . . . holy. (Deuteronomy 26:15, Isaiah 57:15)
- . . . the dwelling place of God. (Matthew 6:9)
- . . . the place where saints are rewarded. (Matthew 5:12)
- . . . a place of indescribable happiness. (Revelation 7:16–17)
- . . . paradise. (2 Corinthians 12:2, 4)
- . . . the kingdom of God. (Ephesians 5:5)

In our culture, it's very common for people to comfort someone grieving the death of a loved one by saying that he or she is "in a better place now." But that doesn't begin to describe the beauty and the glory of the place we call heaven.

✝ Faith in Action

Believers can take comfort in knowing that they have an eternal home and a place of reward with God in heaven.

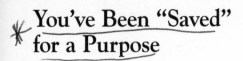

You've Been "Saved" for a Purpose

> *"It is a shame for a person to have been a Christian for years but not to have advanced beyond the knowledge of his salvation."*
>
> —Theodore Epp

John Newton, who wrote one of the best known and most loved Christian hymns, "Amazing Grace," was an amazing example of the transforming power of Jesus Christ. Prior to his conversion around 1748, he truly was, even by the standards of that time, a moral wretch. Newton was the commander of a British slave ship. After his conversion, Newton didn't leave the slave trade right away, but he saw to it that the human cargo on the ships was treated more humanely. Eventually, he realized the immorality of the slave trade and left the seas for good. In the latter half of his life, he became active in the abolitionist movement, influencing British antislavery activists.

Newton understood that God hadn't just saved him and forgiven him, but also wanted to change him. "I am not what I ought to be," he said. "I am not what

I want to be. I am not what I hope to be. But still, I am not what I used to be. And by the grace of God, I am what I am." Newton understood that God had called him to preach the truth of Jesus Christ and to help bring an end to the practice of slavery in the British Empire. Indeed, God has forgiven and cleansed everyone who comes to faith in Jesus Christ. But He doesn't just leave us here on earth to continue in our old lives until we go to heaven. When God saves us, He calls us to grow in our faith through "spiritual disciplines" such as prayer, Bible reading, and fellowship with other Christians and to live lives that in every way point the world's eyes toward the forgiveness Jesus Christ came to bring.

✝ Faith in Action

There is nothing we can do to add to the forgiveness and salvation we receive when we put our faith in Christ. But God has plenty for us to do to make sure that we influence others for Him.

Give Credit Where
Credit Is Due

"Father, glorify your name!"
—Jesus Christ (John 12:28)

In the University of Illinois Fighting Illini's run to the 2005 NCAA championship game, one player in particular established a reputation for himself as one who gives his God the glory for everything that happened on the court.

Roger Powell Jr., a senior forward on the UI team and an ordained minister of the Gospel, became well known for giving Jesus Christ the credit whenever he was interviewed following a game. After one contest in particular—Illinois' near-miraculous come-from-behind overtime win over Arizona—television cameras caught Powell in just such a moment.

"It's what it is! It's Jesus! It's Jesus!" Powell exclaimed to a national television audience while pointing at his shoes, which were covered with Scripture references. In the excitement following the Illini's win, which sent Powell's team to the Final Four in St. Louis, he remembered to give God the glory due Him.

When we talk about glorifying God, we're talking about giving Him the credit through our words and actions for everything. That, the apostle Paul told us, is why He leaves us here on this earth in the first place: "So whether you eat or drink or *whatever you do*, do it all for the glory of God." (1 Corinthians 10:31, italics added)

When we think about glorifying God in our words and deeds, it's good to remember the things God has done for us. Ephraem of Syria, a fourth-century theologian and prolific writer, wrote a poem that lists the wonderful things God has done for us and does for us daily. Part of this poem reads:

> What shall I give you, Lord, in return for
>   all Your kindness?
> Glory to You for Your love.
> Glory to You for Your mercy.
> Glory to You for Your patience.

✝ Faith in Action

Our God is a God who freely pours out His blessings on us every day we walk with Him. When we keep our focus on the fact that all the good things we do and receive are because of Him, we can't help but deflect the credit to Him when others recognize how richly we are blessed.

Part 13

Perseverance

✗ Embracing Disappointment

> *"Trust in yourself and you are doomed to disappointment; . . . but trust in God, and you are never to be confounded in time or eternity."*
> —Dwight L. Moody

None of us can go through life without suffering some kind of disappointment—disappointment with others, disappointment over our circumstances, disappointment with ourselves, even disappointment with God Himself.

The apostle James even went so far as to say that we should be grateful for our times in the valleys: *"Consider it pure joy, my brothers, whenever you face trials of many kinds, because you know that the testing of your faith develops perseverance. Perseverance must finish its work so that you may be mature and complete, not lacking anything."* (James 1:2–4, italics added)

Notice that James doesn't say we should consider it pure joy if we encounter various trials but when we encounter them. We always need to remember that the Christian life isn't all mountaintop times but that we will spend some times in life's valleys as well. But we also need to remember that much good can come from those times where we're tempted to give in to discouragement.

Sometimes our disappointments are rooted in our thinking that we've done something to displease God, and sometimes our disappointment is with God Himself. But that comes from a misunderstanding of God and His love for us. Our Father in heaven loves us so deeply and so completely that there is nothing He won't do to bring us to a point of total dependence on and surrender to Him. Sometimes that means allowing—and, yes, even bringing—disappointments in our lives.

C. S. Lewis made this very point when he wrote, "While what we call 'our own life' remains agreeable, we will not surrender it to Him. What then can God do in our interests but make 'our own life' less agreeable to us?"

✝ Faith in Action

The psalmist David wrote, "When I called, you answered me; you made me bold and stouthearted." (Psalm 138:3) God may or may not change the circumstances that lead to our disappointment. What He absolutely will do, however, is give us the strength to walk with Him through our personal valleys.

Find the Strengths in Weakness

> *"Deny your weakness, and you will never realize God's strength in you."*
>
> —Joni Eareckson Tada

It has been said that Christianity is a religion of paradoxes. One of the greatest paradoxes of our faith is found in the writings of the apostle Paul, who tells us that it is only when we recognize our own weaknesses that God can make us strong: " . . . I will boast all the more gladly about my weaknesses, so that Christ's power may rest on me. That is why, for Christ's sake, I delight in weaknesses, in insults, in hardships, in persecutions, in difficulties. For when I am weak, then I am strong." (2 Corinthians 12:9–10)

"When I am weak, then I am strong" sounds like a direct contradiction until we understand God's purposes for reminding us that without Him we are weak and powerless. That is exactly the lesson the apostle Peter demonstrated for us when he vowed never to abandon Jesus as He faced arrest and crucifixion but later denied him three times.

Peter was the bold and impetuous apostle, the one who dared to do and say what the others would not. But his problem was that he relied on his own strength and courage when Jesus wanted him to understand that he should rely on the power he would receive from the Holy Spirit. Later, Peter would boldly and courageously lead as he worked to establish the church in Jerusalem, but that would happen only after he was humbled to the point of knowing that without God's strength, he truly could do nothing for His kingdom.

One day a friend of James Hudson Taylor, the great missionary to China, complimented him on the impact of his work. Taylor replied, "It seemed to me that God looked over the whole world to find a man who was weak enough to do His work, and when He at last found me, He said, 'He is weak enough—he'll do.'"

Taylor was a man who understood the need to acknowledge his own weakness—and the blessings when he did just that.

† Faith in Action

Faith means believing that God is more than enough to overcome every one of our weaknesses.

Avoid Temptation

"I cannot tell how I am buffeted sometimes by tempta-
tion. . . . Yet I do know that I love God and love His
work, and desire to serve Him only and in all things.
And I value above all else that precious Savior in whom
alone I can be accepted."

—James Hudson Taylor

Animal traders who trap animals in Africa for
American zoos report that one of the most difficult animals to capture is the ringtailed monkey.
For the native Zulus, however, catching these creatures is a simple matter of knowing what it takes to
tempt them.

The Zulus know that one of the ringtailed monkey's favorite foods is watermelon seeds, so they trap
them by setting out a melon with a hole cut in it just
large enough for a monkey to stick its paw into and
grasp the seeds. A monkey will stick its paw into the
melon, grasp as many seeds as it can, then try to pull
its paw out, only to find that it can't because the hole
is too small for its clenched fist to pass through. The
monkey will stubbornly struggle with the melon for

hours, refusing to give up the seeds, even as the Zulus sneak up and nab it.

Just as the Zulus know how to capture a ringtailed monkey by using its weakness for watermelon seeds, the devil knows how to ensnare us by tempting us with the sins he knows are our own personal weaknesses. But we are not left at Satan's mercy when it comes to temptation. As Paul wrote, "God is faithful; he will not let you be tempted beyond what you can bear. But when you are tempted, he will also provide a way out so that you can stand up under it." (1 Corinthians 10:14)

For the Christian, fighting temptation isn't a matter of having more willpower or of simply trying harder. It's a matter of using what the apostle Paul called "the sword of the spirit" (Ephesians 6:17)—the written Word of God—against the devil, who has no defense against what God has said.

✝ Faith in Action

God promised to provide us with everything we need to live lives that please Him, and that includes a devastating weapon against the temptations by the devil: His own written Word.

✳Hang In There for Good

*"He who breathes into our hearts the heavenly
hope, will not deceive or fail us when we press
forward to its realization."*

—Anonymous

After meeting with former slave traders who had
converted to Christianity and were now opposed
to the slave trade, William Wilberforce, a member of
the British Parliament, became convinced that he
should concentrate his efforts in Parliament on the
abolition of the slave trade throughout the Empire.

Beginning in 1788, he submitted draft after draft
of legislation to abolish the slave trade, only to see
them defeated. He was regularly criticized in Parliament and mocked in the newspapers.

But Wilberforce wouldn't give up. He—along
with the Clapham Sect, a group of men devoted to
prayer, Bible study, and mutual encouragement—continued their crusade. Each year for eighteen years,
Wilberforce brought up the issue for a vote. Finally,
on March 25, 1807, the British Empire formally abolished the slave trade.

Having won this victory, Wilberforce set his sights on the abolition of slavery itself. Again, he faced opposition in Parliament, and again he refused to give up. He continued submitting bills abolishing slavery, and on July 26, 1833, three days before his death, he received word that the House of Commons had passed a law freeing all slaves in Britain's colonies.

Upon hearing this news, Wilberforce exclaimed, "Thank God that I have lived to witness the day in which England is willing to give £20 million for the abolishment of slavery." A month later, Parliament formally passed the Slavery Abolition, which gave all slaves in the British Empire their freedom.

God promises us that if we refuse to give up, there will be results: "Let us not become weary in doing good, for at the proper time we will reap a harvest if we do not give up." (Galatians 6:9)

✝ Faith in Action

Few of us will face a situation where we'll need the kind of perseverance and patience William Wilberforce demonstrated. But in each of our lives will come times when doing what is good and right will mean hanging in there and keeping our eyes on God and on the ultimate prize He puts before us.

Suffer Gladly

> "God had one Son on earth without sin,
> but never one without suffering."
>
> —Augustine of Hippo

It's difficult for many believers to associate their faith with suffering, but the Bible tells us that suffering could—and likely will—be a part of our walk of faith. Each of us at some point in our lives will have to endure some kind of suffering, be it because of our own actions, the actions of others, or simply because we live in a fallen world filled with suffering.

When we humans suffer, our natural response is to ask, "Why me?" or, "What have I done to deserve this?" While it is often important to examine ourselves to see what role we play in our suffering, it is equally if not more important to ask, "God, what do you want to do in me through my suffering?"

God doesn't always relieve us in our suffering—at least not right away, and sometimes not in this life—but He always wants to use it for our benefit. The apostle Paul went so far as to encourage believers to be grateful for the suffering they must endure, simply because they build character: "Not only so, but we also rejoice in our sufferings, because we know that suffering produces perseverance; perseverance, character; and character, hope. And hope does not disappoint us, because God has poured out his love into our hearts by the Holy Spirit, whom he has given us." (Romans 5:3–5)

✝ Faith in Action

God has never asked any of us to force ourselves to enjoy our physical, emotional, or spiritual suffering. What He has told us, though, is that if we are surrendered to Him, He can actually use our suffering to make us better people.

Part 14

Charity

✳ Use Money as God's Voice

*"Give according to your income, lest God make your
income according to your giving."*

—Peter Marshall

Someone once asked a very wealthy man how he
could give so much money to the Lord's work but
still have so much personal wealth. The man replied,
"Oh, as I shovel it out, He shovels it in, and the Lord
has a bigger shovel."

Many people are uncomfortable with the subject
of money, particularly when it has to do with issues of
faith. But the Bible has a lot to say about money and
how we are to handle it. One of the best known, and
also probably one of the most misquoted, scripture
verses about money is this: "For the love of money is a
root of all kinds of evil. Some people, eager for money,
have wandered from the faith and pierced themselves
with many griefs." (1 Timothy 6:10)

Nowhere in the Bible is hard work for the purpose of acquiring wealth either discouraged or con-
demned. On the contrary, we are encouraged to work
hard and honestly so that we may have wealth to

share with others: "He who has been stealing must steal no longer, but must work, doing something useful with his own hands, that he may have something to share with those in need." (Ephesians 4:28)

One of the most prevalent—if not *the* most prevalent—biblical themes concerning money is that we are to be generous with what God gives us. Jesus spoke a great deal on the subject of giving. For example, He said, "Give, and it will be given to you. A good measure, pressed down, shaken together and running over, will be poured into your lap. For with the measure you use, it will be measured to you." (Luke 6:38)

✝ Faith in Action

God wants to bless us in all ways, including financially. But He doesn't do that so we can hoard the good things He gives us; rather, He wants us to demonstrate the same kind of generosity He Himself pours out on us. When we do that, we will find that there is no way we can outdo Him when it comes to giving.

✳Jesus: Our Passover Lamb

> *"Learn to sing to [Jesus] and say, 'Lord Jesus, you are my righteousness, I am your sin. You have taken upon yourself what is mine and given me what is yours. You became what you were not, so that I might become what I was not.'"*
>
> —Martin Luther

A small boy made a habit of coming home from school well past the deadline his parents had set for him. One day, he came home even later than usual.

When the boy joined his parents at the dinner table, his plate held nothing but a slice of bread. Next to his plate was a glass of water. He looked over at his father's plate, which was filled with meat and potatoes. Both the mother and father remained silent, waiting for the realization to sink in that this was punishment.

When the father was satisfied that his son understood what was happening, he reached over and took the boy's plate and set it in front of himself. He then took his own plate and set it in front of his son, then smiled at him and told him to eat while he himself had the bread. After that evening, the boy was no longer late coming home. But more important, he saw an illustration of what God had done for him when He sent His Son to take the punishment for his sin.

The apostle Paul referred to Jesus' substitutionary death on the cross for our sins when he wrote, "Get rid of the old yeast that you may be a new batch without yeast—as you really are. For Christ, *our Passover lamb*, has been sacrificed." (1 Corinthians 5:7, italics added)

At the time of the Exodus, a stubborn pharaoh refused to release the Israelites from Egyptian bondage, and God sent a series of plagues. But before He did, He instructed His people to kill a lamb and then spread the blood on their doorposts so that death would "pass over" their homes.

Faith in Action

When Jesus died a horrible death on a Cross, He willingly took the punishment that was rightly ours, giving us forgiveness, salvation, and an eternal home in heaven with God.

✳Change Your Life

> *"Preach the gospel every day; if necessary, use words."*
> —St. Francis of Assisi

In the 1990s a slogan began appearing on bumper stickers, wristbands, T-shirts, and countless other places. It posed the simple question, "What Would Jesus Do?" which was meant to remind believers that they should consider what Jesus' words and actions would have been had He faced their own everyday life situations.

The Bible tells us that God's number-one priority for believers is that they become more and more like Jesus: "For those God foreknew he also predestined to be conformed to the likeness of his Son, that he might be the firstborn among many brothers." (Romans 8:29) In other words, when we follow Jesus, we'll become more and more like him every day.

What does the Bible tell us of Jesus' character and the actions that followed it so perfectly? Here are just a few examples:

Jesus was and is . . .

- . . . holy in His every word and action. (Luke 1:35)
- . . . perfectly righteous in a world full of unrighteousness. (Hebrews 1:19)
- . . . faithful to Himself and His Father. (1 Thessalonians 5:24)
- . . . just in His judgments because He followed the will of the Father. (John 5:30)
- . . . without sin, though He was tempted. (Matthew 4:1–10)
- . . . obedient to His Father in every way. (John 15:10)
- . . . merciful to all repentant sinners. (Hebrews 2:17)

God never intended that our faith in Jesus Christ be just a ticket to heaven when we die but that through Him we enter into a relationship with God that changes us from the inside out. He wants the world to see in us reflections of every part of Christ's character. He wants our every deed come from our desire to be imitators of Jesus.

✝ Faith in Action

Being a Christian means being more and more like Jesus every day of our walk with Him. That means doing the things He did, thinking the things He thought, and being submitted to the will of God.

Give Meaning to Your Work

"It is not what a man does that determines whether his work is sacred or secular, but why he does it."

—A. W. Tozer

In early 1901, the U.S. Steel Corporation took over Carnegie Steel, which was founded by Andrew Carnegie. As part of the takeover agreement, U.S. Steel inherited as one of its obligations a contract to pay the top Carnegie executive, Charles M. Schwab, the then-unheard-of base salary of $1,000,000.

This was quite a predicament for J. P. Morgan of U.S. Steel. The highest salary on record was then $100,000, and he knew that continuing to pay Schwab what he had been making would endanger the corporation's chances of being competitive. Morgan met with Schwab, showed him the contract, and asked what could be done about it. "This!" Schwab said, then tore up the contract, which had paid him a total of $1.3 million the previous year.

Schwab later told a *Forbes* magazine interviewer: "I was not animated by money motives. I believed in what I was trying to do and I wanted to see it brought about."[12]

A lot of people, including many believers, see work as a burden, as something they *have* to do in order to pay the bills and find little or no satisfaction in what they do. They equate work with words like *toil*, or *drudgery*. But that is not how God wants us to see work.

God was the One who invented the work, and He first put humans to work way back in the Garden of Eden: "The Lord God took the man and put him in the Garden of Eden to work it and take care of it." (Genesis 2:15)

Sadly, too many believers tend to compartmentalize their lives. There is the work part, the family part, and the "religious" part. But our God wants it all to be part of our worship.

✝ Faith in Action

God wants us to do whatever work we do as if we're doing it directly for Him. When we do that, we will see our work as a true blessing from God.

✳Sow Seeds of Love

"God has created me to do him some definite service;
he has committed some work to me which he has not
committed to another. I have my mission—I never may
know it in this life, but I shall be told it in the next."
                                    —John Henry Newman

St. Francis of Assisi was an amazing Christian man who lived and ministered to the poorest of the poor in Italy in the third century.

Francis, whose given name was Giovanni Francesco Bernardone, was born in Assisi, a town about midway down the Italian peninsula. Francis was part of a wealthy family. But, following a stint in the military and some time in a prisoner of war camp, Francis began taking his faith more seriously than he had before.

In the winter of 1208, Francis attended a Mass where he heard the account of Jesus' sending His disciples out to preach, telling them, "Do not take along any gold or silver or copper in your belts; take no bag for the journey, or extra tunic, or sandals or a staff; for the worker is worth his keep." (Matthew 10:9–10)

Francis took Jesus' instructions very personally and very literally, and he left Assisi with nothing more than the tunic on his back and embraced a life of simplicity and poverty as he ministered to the poorest of the poor and the sickest of the sick. Later he, along with two men who came to be called Brother Bernard and Brother Peter, started a movement that became known as the Franciscans.

In addition to caring for the poor, Francis did a lot of writing. That writing included a prayer of devotion to service to God and humankind that came to be known as "The Prayer of St. Francis."

✝ Faith in Action

God doesn't call all of us to live a life of poverty like the one St. Francis of Assisi embraced. He does, however, call us to service, to be instruments for His use. Like St. Francis, each of us has been put here to minister to those around us, to sow love, forgiveness, faith, hope, light, and joy in a world desperately needing all of them.

Part 15

Fellowship

Gather in His Name

> *"Christianity without discipleship is always*
> *Christianity without Christ."*
> —Dietrich Bonhoeffer

Jesus' challenge to "take up your cross daily and follow me" (Luke 9:23) was His call to discipleship, which we can define as committing ourselves to following Him every day with everything we have. But we can also define discipleship as giving up our own desires and goals in exchange for the eternal blessings promised those who wholeheartedly follow Christ.

Many believers wonder what exactly is involved in discipleship. They know they can't physically follow Jesus the way the disciples did. But they also know that Jesus calls each of us to follow Him with everything we have. Today, following Jesus looks very much the same as it did when He was alive on earth in that it means commitment to doing the things it takes to remain close to Him and grow in Him.

Dawson Trotman, who in 1934 founded the Navigators—an international outreach ministry to college campuses, military bases, inner cities, prisons, and youth camps—defined discipleship using his own "Wheel Illustration," in which the wheel represented the whole of our own lives. In it, the hub of the wheel is Jesus Himself; just as the hub of a wheel is its center, so is Jesus to be the center of our lives as His disciples.

The four spokes of the wheel represent four essentials for growth in the Christian life: prayer, Bible reading and study, fellowship with other believers, and witnessing to those who need to hear the message of Jesus Christ.

God never intended for any of us to go it alone when it comes to growing as Jesus' disciples, and He has provided for us the means to that growth. Through prayer and reading His written Word, the Bible, we get to know Him better and grow in our faith in Him. Through fellowship with other believers, we receive encouragement and motivation to continue in that growth.

Faith in Action

Through witnessing to others about the wonderful things Jesus has done for us—and continues to do—we have the opportunity to give back to Him who has given us the very best He has.

✳ Remember You Are Holy

> *"The Church is a society of sinners—the only society in the world in which membership is based upon the single qualification that the candidate shall be unworthy of membership."*
>
> —Charles C. Morrison

Groucho Marx once said, "I refuse to join any club that would have me as a member." In other words, if a club's standards for admittance were that low, Marx wanted nothing to do with it.

Those of us who follow Jesus Christ as our Lord and Savior are part of a club—God's eternal family—filled with people who appear, at least in human understanding, to be completely unworthy of organizations with the very lowest standards of admission. God has infinitely high standards for admittance—standards none of us could reach, no matter how good our lives may appear.

God's one standard for admittance into His kingdom is this: absolute holiness. That means lives that are 100 percent pleasing to Him, lives that are without sin or imperfection of any kind. And in and of ourselves, there is nothing that makes us worthy of God's love or worthy to be a part of His family. Furthermore, there is nothing we can do and nothing we can say that makes us any more—or less—acceptable in God's eyes.

At a glance, that looks like a pretty hopeless situation for all of us. But while the Bible teaches that we are all sinners worthy of God's judgment, it also teaches us that God poured out His love on us anyway when He sent Jesus Christ to be a once-and-for-all sacrifice for our sin. And when we place our faith in Christ, God declares that we are not just forgiven but Holy in His sight.

God calls each of His children to live holy lives. But He doesn't make our own sinlessness a prerequisite for entrance into His kingdom. Rather, He takes us as we are, draws us close to Him, then empowers us to live lives that are pleasing to Himself.

✝ Faith in Action

We aren't justified in God's sight by whatever righteousness we can muster; instead, we are able to live holy lives because He has already justified us.

Part 16

Compassion

❋ Bite Your Tongue

> *"Never believe anything bad about anybody unless you positively know it to be true; never tell even that unless you feel that it is absolutely necessary—and that God is listening while you tell it."*
>
> —William Penn

One day, a woman known for being a gossip visited the offices of the *Chicago Daily News*. She was wearing a white dress and inadvertently leaned against a wall where a freshly printed copy of the front page was hanging, and some of the print came off on the back of her white dress.

Later, as the woman walked down the street to meet her husband, she noticed that people walking behind her were snickering. When she reached the place where her husband was waiting, she asked him if there was anything on her back that shouldn't be there. As she turned around, he read the large black reversed letters: sweN yliaD. He replied, "No, dear, nothing's on your back that doesn't belong there."[13]

Gossip ruins friendships, reputations, ministries, and other human relationships. Make no mistake, our words can hurt others. The Bible has plenty to say about the sin of gossip. In the book of Proverbs alone, we find these warnings:

- "A gossip betrays a confidence, but a trustworthy man keeps a secret." (Proverbs 11:13)
- "A perverse man stirs up dissension, and a gossip separates close friends." (Proverbs 16:28)
- "The words of a gossip are like choice morsels; they go down to a man's inmost parts." (Proverbs 18:8)
- "A gossip betrays a confidence; so avoid a man who talks too much." (Proverbs 20:19)
- "Without wood a fire goes out; without gossip a quarrel dies down." (Proverbs 16:20)

The apostle Paul also warned believers about the destructiveness of gossip: " . . . they get into the habit of being idle and going about from house to house. And not only do they become idlers, but also gossips and busybodies, saying things they ought not to." (1 Timothy 5:13)

✝ Faith in Action

Think before you talk. And if what you are thinking of saying isn't true, helpful, and kind, just bite your tongue.

✳ Pay It Forward for God

> *"A Christian should always remember that the value*
> *of his good works is not based on their number*
> *and excellence, but on the love of God which*
> *prompts him to do these things."*
> —Juan de la Cruz (John of the Cross)

Jesus' life on earth was all about compassion—compassion for the sick, the poor, the lame, the outcasts, and sinners. In other words, compassion for all of humankind.

Jesus not only demonstrated compassion in His own words and deeds, but He also instructed His followers to do the same, telling them, " . . . whatever you did for one of the least of these brothers of mine, you did for me." (Matthew 25:40)

But who are the "least of these brothers"?

In His earthly ministry, Jesus Himself demonstrated what it means to "do for the least of these brothers" as He reached out to everyone who came near Him—all without regard to their social or religious standing. We should be challenged to do the very same thing in our own worlds today.

The apostle James wrote, "In the same way, faith by itself, if it is not accompanied by action, is dead. But someone will say, 'You have faith; I have deeds.' Show me your faith without deeds, and I will show you my faith by what I do." (2:17–18) In short, if you have true faith in God, it will be reflected in the things that you do—for Him and for others.

None of us makes ourselves right with God by any good thing we do. Our acts of charity and compassion, no matter how profoundly they relieve the suffering of the neediest among us, mean nothing in God's eyes if they are not motivated by our faith in and love for Him.

Those of us who identify ourselves as followers of Jesus Christ are the beneficiaries of the greatest act of love and compassion in human history. As such, we can't help but make ourselves vessels of that love and compassion to those around us.

✝ Faith in Action

Look around you today and see who in your circle of influence could use a kind word or act of compassion.

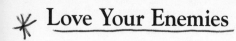

✳ Love Your Enemies

"I choose kindness . . . I will be kind to the poor,
for they are alone. Kind to the rich,
for they are afraid. And kind to the unkind,
for such is how God has treated me."

—Max Lucado

Peter Miller was a Baptist pastor who lived in Ephrata, Pennsylvania, at the time of the American Revolution. Also living in Ephrata was Michael Wittman, who constantly went out of his way to oppose and humiliate Miller.

Wittman was arrested for treason, tried, and sentenced to death. Miller was a close friend of General George Washington, and when he had learned of Wittman's death sentence, he traveled seventy miles to Philadelphia on foot to plead with Washington for the traitor's life.

"No, Peter," General Washington said. "I cannot grant you the life of your friend."

"My friend!" exclaimed the preacher. "He's the bitterest enemy I have."

"You've walked seventy miles to save the life of an enemy?' asked an incredulous Washington. "That puts the matter in a different light. I'll grant your pardon."

Peter Miller walked back to Ephrata, this time with Michael Wittman at his side.[14]

For most people, it would seem unthinkable to plead the case of someone who had intentionally done us wrong. But the Bible tells us that is exactly what we are to do.

Jesus did more than talk the talk when it came to loving His enemies; He walked the walk—all the way to the Cross. Jesus endured horrific treatment at the hands of those who had opposed Him. But He did so willingly, because that is what the Father had sent Him to do. And as He hung in agony on that cross of wood, He pleaded with God on behalf of His tormenters: "Father, forgive them, for they do not know what they are doing." (Luke 23:34)

✝ Faith in Action

Jesus set the perfect example of how we should deal with those who mistreat us, even when they do it intentionally. When we look at that example, how can we do any less for those we come into contact with every day?

God's Great Mercy

"God's mercy with a sinner is only equaled and perhaps outmatched by His patience with the saints, with you and me."

—Alan Redpath

God's mercy is based on the fact that He is a merciful God who desires to pour mercy out on those who fully realize that they don't deserve it.

The Bible is a book all about God's mercy. It constantly reminds us that while we may do things that hurt us and our relationship with a holy God, He will always be merciful to us when we come to Him acknowledging that we deserve anything but.

King David wrote of this amazing mercy in several of his psalms. That included these words: "The Lord has heard my cry for mercy; the Lord accepts my prayer." (Psalm 6:9)

Later on in Israel's history, the people saw an example of God extending His mercy to a rebellious people who cried out to Him. Speaking through the prophet Isaiah during a time in Israel's history when, because of the people's great sin against God, they were held captive by the Babylonians, God reminded His people that though they had to endure difficult times, He had not and would not forget them: "For a brief moment I abandoned you, but with deep compassion I will bring you back. In a surge of anger I hid my face from you for a moment, but with everlasting kindness I will have compassion on you." (Isaiah 54:7, 8)

The Bible tells us that God's mercy for us is great, (Numbers 14:18) rich, (Ephesians 2:4) abundant, (1 Peter 1:3) sure, (Micah 7:20) everlasting, (Psalm 136) and constantly renewable. (Lamentations 3:23)

Mercy is why God keeps us alive and cares for us, even when we neglect Him.

Mercy is why God sustained and forgave an often-rebellious nation of Israel through thousands of years of ups and downs.

✝ Faith in Action

Mercy is why God sent His Son, Jesus Christ, so that we could find free forgiveness for our sins and could find fellowship with the Father, even though there is nothing about us that makes us worthy of Him.

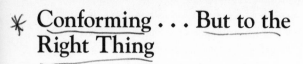

Conforming . . . But to the Right Thing

> *"The opposite of bravery is not cowardice,*
> *but conformity."*
>
> —Robert Anthony

In his book *Living above the Level of Mediocrity,* Charles R. Swindoll illustrated the dangers of conformity using the story of a highly intelligent but still foolish fly:

> Once a spider built a beautiful web in an old house. He kept it clean and shiny so that flies would patronize it. The minute he got a "customer" he would clean up on him so the other flies would not get suspicious. Then one day this fairly intelligent fly came buzzing by the clean spider web. Old man spider called out, "Come in and sit." But the fairly intelligent fly said, "No, sir. I don't see other flies in your house, and I am not going in alone!" But presently he saw on the floor below a large crowd of flies dancing around on a piece of brown paper.

He was delighted! He was not afraid if lots of flies were doing it. So he came in for a landing. Just before he landed, a bee zoomed by, saying, "Don't land there, stupid! That's flypaper!" But the fairly intelligent fly shouted back, "Don't be silly. Those flies are dancing. There's a big crowd there. Everybody's doing it. That many flies can't be wrong!" Well, you know what happened. He died on the spot. Some of us want to be with the crowd so badly that we end up in a mess. What does it profit a fly (or a person) if he escapes the web only to end up in the glue?[15]

✝ Faith in Action

The apostle Paul wrote, "For those God foreknew he also predestined to be conformed to the likeness of his Son, that he might be the firstborn among many brothers." (Romans 8:29) In other words, we are to conform ourselves, but we are to conform ourselves to Jesus Christ, who refused to go along with the crowd.

Notes

1. *Progress* magazine, December 14, 1992.

2. *The Supremacy of Jesus*, Stephen Neill, Inter-Varsity Press, 1984, pp. 79–80.

3. *Today in the Word*, March 14, 1991.

4. *Through the Valley of the Kwai*, Ernest Gordon, Wipf & Stock Publishers, 1997.

5. *The Book of 750 Bible and Gospel Studies*, George W. Noble, 1909.

6. *The Billy Graham Christian Worker's Handbook*, Billy Graham, World Wide Publications, 1984, pp. 53–54.

7. *Bits & Pieces*, October 15, 1992, p. 13.

8. *Present Day Parables*, J. Wilbur Chapman, F. M. Barton, 1900.

9. *The Wycliffe Handbook of Preaching and Preachers*, Warren W. Wiersbe, Moody Publishers, 1984, p. 211.

10. *A Slow and Certain Light: Thoughts on the Guidance of God*, Elisabeth Elliot, Word Books, 1973.

11. *Little House on the Freeway*, Tim Kimmel, Multnomah, 1994, pp. 41–42.

12. *Bits & Pieces*, May 1991, p. 2.

13. *Our Daily Bread*, June 23, 1994.

14. *The Grace of Giving*, Stephen F. Olford, Zondervan Publishing House, 1972.

15. *Living above the Level of Mediocrity*, Charles R. Swindoll, W Publishing Group, 1989, pp. 223–224.

About the Authors

James Stuart Bell has served for many years as editorial director at Moody Press. He has received cover credit for more than fifteen books that he compiled, edited, or introduced. He is editor of Alpha Books' *Christian Family Guide* series. Before joining Moody Press, he was the Director of Religious Publishing at Doubleday in New York. He is also the author of *Just Add Jesus, A Cup of Comfort Devotional,* and *A Cup of Comfort Devotional for Women.* Jim earned his B.A. in English from Holy Cross College in Massachusetts, and his M.A. in English Literature from University College in Dublin. He lives in Chicago, IL.

Tracy Macon Sumner is a freelance writer who has coauthored *The Complete Idiot's Guide to Jesus* and *The Complete Idiot's Guide to the Reformation and Protestantism* with James Stuart Bell. He lives in Lake Oswego, OR.